THE WEST SIDE WALTZ

ERNEST THOMPSON

THE WEST SIDE WALTZ

A Play in 3/4 Time

With an Introduction by
KATHARINE HEPBURN

DODD, MEAD & COMPANY · NEW YORK

FIRST EDITION

PHOTOGRAPHS BY STEVE SCHAPIRO

Library of Congress Cataloging in Publication Data

Thompson, Ernest, 1949–
    The West Side Waltz.

    I. Title.
PS3570.H599W4   812'.54   82-2501
ISBN 0-396-08061-8   AACR2

*Dedicated to George Seaton, whose talent and films
are legendary, and whose generosity and belief
in a new writer were invaluable and inspiring*

INTRODUCTION

Ernest Thompson is a comparatively new member of the Writer's Guild. And they are the ones who dominate the theater and the movies and the books we read. We've been through a period of play writing where the main concern has been the extraordinary—not the *hero* type, the *freak* type. The great central mass of humanity—male, female, young, old, medium—has been left as an uninteresting sort of not-worth-thinking-about group. They live, they die, and they don't stimulate pen to paper. Or ribbon to type. They are the dull ones whom the *freaks* beat up on, murder, impose upon.

As most of us are members of this mass group, we have a right to feel neglected.

Ernest Thompson is bringing the ordinary human back to life. He is making him/her fun to be with. This is what appeals to me so much in his writing. It is a warm delight to people to see themselves and their very real and simple problems brought to the fore with humor and with sensitivity. And if you're an actor it is this sort of part that is most appealing to play. At least that is what I think. You can strike right through to the vulnerable core of many members of the audience. And they are moved. Or they laugh. But most important—they feel understood.

It is very important for people to feel understood. Most lives are tough. One long struggle. But the problems we face—although our circumstances are quite different—seem to be curiously similar.

In *On Golden Pond* and in *The West Side Waltz* a group of average humans are gathered together with a warmth and humor and understanding that are sheer delight. The young, medium, old, very old, sick, well. Living in perfectly regulation-American circumstances. You are taken along with them to observe what could be a period of time in any of our lives. He reveals them to us with an incredible sensitivity, a delicious humor, and a remarkable sense of words and rhythms.

From whence cometh all this wisdom and delight?

I was amazed when I first met him. Very early thirties. Tall, athletic, handsome—really quite something in the dreamiest sense of the word. Yes. Fast cars, speedboats.

He was an actor.

Where in the world did he pick up his really extraordinary knowledge?

Well he did. And it has happened. And he is astounded and thrilled too. As a child is thrilled when he wins the race. No false sophistication in his attitude. Just beaming *joy*. They like me. I can do it!

Oh, *life! Life!*

Wasn't I lucky to run into him. That's what I'm thinking. And that's what his ever-increasing public is thinking. There is something enormously healthy about laughing at one's self. It helps you to pull yourself together and to march on down the road of life, which is as we all know chock-full of hurdles.

But wait!

There's a bright spot!
Where?
Over there. See it. Oh, no. It's gone. But just keep looking.
To me his contribution is uplifting.

New York City
February 1982

Katharine Hepburn and Dorothy Loudon

Regina Baff and Don Howard

Dorothy Loudon

David Margulies and Don Howard

THE WEST SIDE WALTZ *had its world premiere at the Spreckles Theatre, San Diego, California, on December 20, 1980, and was presented by Robert Whitehead and Roger L. Stevens, in association with Center Theatre-Ahmanson (Robert Fryer, producer), at the Ethel Barrymore Theatre, New York City, on November 19, 1981.*

CARA VARNUM	*Dorothy Loudon*
SERGE BARRESCU	*David Margulies*
MARGARET MARY ELDERDICE	*Katharine Hepburn*
ROBIN BIRD	*Regina Baff*
GLEN DABRINSKY	*Don Howard*

Directed by NOEL WILLMAN
Set design by BEN EDWARDS
Costumes by JANE GREENWOOD
Lighting design by THOMAS SKELTON
Music supervised and arranged by DAVID KRANE

Stravagante, con affetto, con brio

PRELUDE

Violin

Prelude no. 1 by J. S. Bach

(The playing is outrageous. Surges of true inspiration, stretches of getting by, dips into disaster. A mistake is made, returned to, repeated, attempted a third time, mucked up worse than ever, and left where it was. The piece ends with a thud.)

Prelude no. 7 by J. S. Bach

(A little more *legato*, a little more familiar to the musician. However, the piece is interrupted midway, and the strings of the violin are tested and tuned. Then the Prelude no. 7 is brought to a reasonably happy finish.)

Menuetto I and II by Georg Friedrich Handel

(The first is just zipped through, a stunning display of concentration and grace. The bow of the violin, unfortunately enough, is dropped at the end, and an awkward moment passes before the second piece begins. It is a lively number and the playing very nearly rises to the music, though there is confusion audible near the end, and it seems the finish of Menuetto I has found its way into Menuetto II. It works out all right.)

"Neapolitan Nights" by J. S. Zamecnik

(Now here the playing shines, the delivery frolicking and heartfelt, and, when it wavers from the true line of good musical sense, it's hardly noticeable.)

"Du und Du" by Johann Strauss
(This is tricky for some reason. The violinist proceeds boldly for a number of measures, then wanders way wide of the mark, and just gives up.)

"Neapolitan Nights" by J. S. Zamecnik
(It was more fun to begin with, and this time round it's hilarious.)

Etuden no. 1 by Franz Wohlfahrt
(Back to basics, practicing making perfect, or so the theory goes.)

"Du und Du" by Johann Strauss
(The invigoration of drill work has inspired the musician to a heady new effort at "Du und Du," but, unhappily, has not provided a key to the obstacles. The effort fails.)

Etuden no. 2 by Franz Wohlfahrt
(Good going here, in and out in a matter of seconds.)

"Du und Du" by Johann Strauss
(Didn't help. The first several measures and that's it.)

"My Hero" by Johann Strauss
(A piece of cake. Downright slick.)

"Du und Du" by Johann Strauss
(One last try for Mother. The rough spot is reached, and then neatly skipped over, there being more than one way to skin cats. Unfortunately, there's more than one rough spot, and the violinist wisely says, "The hell with it," and segues back to the favorite stretches of:)

"My Hero" by Johann Strauss
(And it's very smartly done.)

ACT ONE

Scene One

"Du und Du" by Johann Strauss

Winter. Afternoon.

*The music continues. We find ourselves in the liv-
ing room of a West Side, New York, apartment, a
huge room with high ceilings and tall windows,
old and odd. The furnishings are eclectic but
related by charm. A grand piano dominates the
space; it is parked stage right, dressed in a lacy
shawl and piled high with sheet music and music
books. Resting on stands beside it are an old acous-
tical guitar and an oboe, both shiny and ready to
go. An empty violin case lies open on a table. Stage
left are several easy chairs in varying repair and
style, and a sofa, tattered at an elbow but patched
with care. Above this sitting area is a thirties vin-
tage birch dining set. Throughout the room there
are various end tables and coffee tables, each bear-
ing one or several curios. There are thin rugs on
the parquet floor, and thick, warm drapes on the
windows. The walls are papered with faded flowers, and where there is wood, around the doors,*

3

and the doors themselves, the window sills and jambs, the wood is dark and handsome, never painted. The room is cluttered and dusty, but comfy and bright.

There is a tiny foyer upstage, with a door on each of its walls, the entrance in the center, a closet to the right, the kitchen to the left. On the upstage wall are two windows and another door to the kitchen. Stage right are four giant windows, through which can be seen corners of other tall buildings, water towers, and sky. The stage left wall has two doors, one mirrored and leading into a small room, the other wooden and opening onto a hallway. Both are closed now. A thin ribbon of sunlight falls from a window. The sky is brilliant blue.

The music plays on. From the kitchen enters the musician, CARA VARNUM. She is rotund, fifty-six, rosy-faced, with odd-colored hair, peach maybe, done up royally with a bow. She wears bright makeup and a neat, flowered dress, covered at the moment by a rather ratty old sweater. She is a bustly person, with great confused quantities of love, concern, and fear.

She is playing jubilantly. "My Hero." Even as she crosses from the kitchen to her perch on the piano bench, she plays. She settles, head tipped to the side, upper torso dipping in time to the music. Her playing is, as we know, competent, good, even daring within the confines of her ability. Not so good beyond it. She's crackling now. She slides to the far

4

edge of the bench where she can stare with great interest at a glass bowl of bonbons on a nearby table. Keeping in rhythm and replacing the strains of her violin with the bright "la-la-la" of her voice, she flits across the space, plucks up a bonbon, pops it into her mouth, and flits back, not a beat missed. She resumes her playing while she chews. After a moment of inspired performing, she again eyes the candy and again sings, flits, plucks, and pops, but this time doesn't sit. Now she walks as she plays and chews. She sashays her way to the window and attempts to fit herself into the thin stream of sunlight, no small task. She looks about, then steps over and hooks with her foot the rung of a dining chair, which she drags back to the window. Now she lowers herself onto it, playing all the while.

She doesn't hear the sickly doorbell ring, not at first. It is only through the persistence of the ringer that CARA's *concentration is broken, and, at last, she looks up and stops. It is with real reluctance that she lowers bow and fiddle and steps to the door, unlocks the locks, and opens up.*

In steps SERGE BARRESCU, *a man of fifty or so, thick face and body, thinning hair, intense, good-natured, up to a point, a gentle smile, and only the most tentative grasp of the English language. He wears blue work trousers and a matching work shirt. His hands are filthy. He grins.*

SERGE

Mrs. Varnum. Always in the wrong place.

5

CARA

Story of my life. Come in, Serge. Close the door. Close it. About time you showed up.

SERGE

This is funny. You got such a nice pretty place, 204. You got you your Sony TV, you little ugly cat, and but now I find you always here, 1506. Why you think?
(She stares at him)

CARA

I have something to say to you and I want you to listen very closely. There's trouble a'brewin'.
(She draws a deep breath, then steps back away from him to the window)
Do you realize that it's practically below freezing in this apartment and my apartment and the whole building? There are roaches dying of frostbite in the kitchen. It's very, very, very cold in here.

SERGE

Well. Is very cold outside.

CARA

Yes, but you see we pay money to live inside. Look at this ratty sweater. It doesn't begin to go with my outfit.
(She steps to the hallway door and listens)
It's not so bad for me anyway, I'm younger and fatter and I can put up with Arctic weather. I'm a walrus. But what about poor Mrs. Elderdice, hmm? Do you know how many elderly people die every day in New York because they freeze to death or starve to death or are run over by taxis, that sort of thing? One thousand!

SERGE

One thousand? Every day?

6

CARA

One thousand! If I hadn't come in here this afternoon and put an extra blanket on her, she might never have woke up at all. It makes me *heartsick.* The cold is very, very, very bad for her.

SERGE

This is something I know. But the broiler is sick.

CARA

Can't you make the broiler well?

SERGE

I don't know.

CARA

(She crosses back to SERGE*)*

I'm going to tell you something and I want you to listen very closely. We have had enough! The owners of this building are niggardly! And they're cheap! And we're taking *action! We're* going to have a *meeting* of the *tenants.* And we're going to type up the minutes and pass them around and send petitions to the manager and we're going to serve refreshments and coffee—I'm going to make sandwiches— and we're going to have floor representatives and things are going to be different. *Right* will *out!*

(She glowers triumphantly at SERGE*)*

SERGE

(Calmly)

Mrs. Varnum, let me tell you something. I know this crazy feeling, but I am the one to fix the broiler, and I fix. Lis-ten—one thousand people dying every day, and in Romania you can't buy Sony TV. Hey. Play this violin, make some pretty music.

7

CARA

I will not play the violin. Who do you think I am, Nero?
Hmm?

SERGE

Mrs. Varnum, play the violin, I promise I go and fix the
heat.
> *(She looks at him, looks at the hallway door. She
> can't resist. She lifts her violin and plays lightly
> her favorite part of "My Hero")*

Ah, goddam, is so *beautiful.* You want to dance?
> *(She shakes her head, attacks the finish of the
> piece with awesome fervor. She plays the final
> notes with such passion she is virtually trembling
> as she lowers the violin.* SERGE *bursts into
> applause.* CARA *smiles, embarrassed and thrilled.*
> SERGE *claps on, louder.* CARA *awkwardly curtsies,
> then curtsies lower, and at this moment the hall-
> way door opens and* MARGARET MARY ELDERDICE
> *enters. She is seventy-three and peppery, a bit off
> balance at the present, a staunch and proud
> woman, always sure of her wants, variable as they
> may be. Her fears, anxieties, loneliness, and most
> other emotions and feelings she keeps neatly bound
> between the veneers of distance and humor. She is
> afflicted with impaired hearing and impaired
> mobility, and other inconveniences, but she gives
> them all a good fight. She is attractive enough by
> nature, and though she does little to enhance what
> she has, she never fails to sparkle. She is dressed
> now in a very plain house dress, covered by a very
> old sweater, her grey hair is on its own, and she
> wears old crocheted slippers. She leans on the door
> frame and regards the spectacle before her)*

8

MARGARET MARY
Well. Aren't you nice? Hello, pumpkin.

CARA
(Straightening and looking sheepish)
Hi, Margaret Mary.

MARGARET MARY
Were you playing? Aren't you a good girl? Practice, practice. Hello, Serge.

SERGE
Miss Elderdice, how you are?

MARGARET MARY
Not bad, thank you.

CARA
Did you sleep well?

MARGARET MARY
For a while. Until an extra blanket mysteriously found its way onto my bed, and I woke up in a muck sweat.
(She starts across the room, moving slowly and with difficulty. She smiles at SERGE*)*
You look pretty sparkly today. No calamities?

SERGE
Thank you.

CARA
You better go, Serge.

MARGARET MARY
What did you say?

9

CARA
(Loudly)
I said Serge had better go. You need your rest.

MARGARET MARY
I've just had my rest.

CARA
Yes, well, he's got places to be. There's trouble a'brewin'.
There's no reason for us to have to wear ratty sweaters.

MARGARET MARY
Cara, sometimes I have no idea what you're talking about.
Serge, I believe there's something wrong with my heat,
think you could fix it?

SERGE
I don't know. I will try.

MARGARET MARY
You're a good boy. You do the building proud.

SERGE
Thank you. Always you have such nice things to say to me,
and to everybody.

CARA
Except me.

MARGARET MARY
What did you say?
*(CARA shrugs and shakes her head. MARGARET
MARY hobbles toward the window. CARA looks at
SERGE and shakes her head again)*

10

CARA

Margaret Mary, Ralphie's sick.

> (MARGARET MARY *doesn't hear, or at least doesn't respond. To* SERGE)

Ralphie is my cat. He's sick.

> (SERGE *nods gravely*)

Know why I call him Ralphie?

> (SERGE *shakes his head*)

Because that's his name.

> (*She giggles*)

SERGE

I understand.

MARGARET MARY
(At the window)

It's a crystal day. Perfect for a walk in the park.

CARA

You can't walk out there today.

MARGARET MARY

I beg your pardon?

CARA
(Stepping toward her and shouting)

It's too cold to walk in the park today.

MARGARET MARY

Then I'll run. Everyone else does. I'll buy a pair of sneakers and a sweatshirt with a dirty slogan and I'll blend right in with the crowd. How about it, Serge? Go for a few quick laps around the reservoir?

11

SERGE

(Laughing)

Miss Elderdice, this is something I like about you very much. You are certainly funny.

MARGARET MARY

Am I? Isn't that nice? I don't feel funny. Look, there she is. Come here and look.
(She waves at CARA *and* SERGE. *They look at each other and step to the window)*
Do you see her? On the bench. The only person sitting still. It's as though she doesn't feel the cold at all.

CARA

She's a bag lady, Margaret Mary. She's too crazy to feel the cold.
(She turns away from the window. SERGE *shakes his head and turns, but* MARGARET MARY *stares, fascinated)*

MARGARET MARY

Have you ever listened to her? She says some of the most remarkable things. Once when I passed her she yelled at me that Jesus was a *thaumaturgist*. I thought it was a gibberish word until I looked in the dictionary. It means "magician." What do you think of that? Rather erudite, wouldn't you say?
*(*CARA *shrugs.* SERGE *smiles)*
I see I'm alone in my fascination with this woman.

SERGE

I going now.

MARGARET MARY

Oh, all right. Come and visit again won't you? It's always a pleasure to see your handsome face.

SERGE

(He starts to go, stops)

Let me tell you something I know. I have been in this country for some time. Since Communists. I have this bad job in this building, and before this, other bad jobs. I have bad apartment and bad wife. I am in United States, the land of the milk and the honey, and still I am unhappy. So, this is life.

MARGARET MARY

What are you going on about?

CARA

(Loudly)

He's not happy.

MARGARET MARY

Oh, I'm sorry.

SERGE

No, is okay. This is what I want to tell. I have not so much money. But I am *lucky*. I have *friends*. Is so wonderful—friends. Miss Elderdice and Mrs. Varnum the best of all.

MARGARET MARY

Serge, don't you ever think about going back to . . . where is it you come from, Poland?

SERGE

Romania, Romania! What for, to be shot? I can be shot in New York and save eight hundred dollars.

13

(He laughs)

This is funny. I going now. Good-bye, Mrs. Varnum, thank you for the music so pretty.

(He bows to them both)

Thank you for being nice.

(He exits)

MARGARET MARY

He's precious, isn't he?

CARA

(Loudly)

He's a moron. He's worse than the last one.

MARGARET MARY

The last what?

CARA

The last super.

MARGARET MARY

The last super. That has an odd sort of ring to it. I like his verve. Although I must say he smells a bit like a pond. Oh, bother, I wanted him to check the rat room. I don't suppose you'd like to stick your head in and see if we have any visitors, would you?

CARA

No!

MARGARET MARY

Well, aren't you the poor sport?

CARA

What did Dr. Cameron have to say?

MARGARET MARY

Dr. Cameron told me I am an old lady, which came as no surprise to me. I've had my suspicions for some time. I was not very impressed with your Dr. Cameron, and I told him as much as I climbed off the table and got dressed.

CARA

He didn't watch you dress, did he?

MARGARET MARY

Yes, he did. He has joined the select fraternity of those who know the glorious truth. Actually, I think he was so depressed at not finding anything spectacular, he couldn't move. They like it better when you have cancer, you know. It gives them a feeling of grandeur.
(She moves across the room)
They *don't really* care, you know.

CARA

You need someone to take care of you.

MARGARET MARY

No, I don't. I see you've decimated the bonbon supply.

CARA

I don't think decimated is the right word.

MARGARET MARY

How about ravaged then?

15

CARA

I thought that was what they were here for.

MARGARET MARY

You thought they were here to ravage?

CARA

I thought they were for your guests, and I'm a guest.

MARGARET MARY

I'd hoped to have others.

CARA

I'd like to know who.

MARGARET MARY

What did you say?

CARA
(Louder)

I'd like to know who you're hoping to have. Not Mrs. Delalagro, that's for sure.

MARGARET MARY
(Strongly)

We'll not mention Mrs. Delalagro again, Cara.

CARA

All right, there's no need to be touchy. I know you're upset. I know what it's like. I was devastated when my mother died suddenly at the age of ninety-one.

MARGARET MARY

No one dies suddenly at the age of ninety-one.

16

CARA

Well, you don't have any friends, that's all I'm saying. The only friends I've known you to have in all the years I've seen you in the building were your husband—

MARGARET MARY
(Interrupting)

He was no friend.

CARA

And Mrs. Delalagro. And they're both dead.

MARGARET MARY

Doesn't speak very well for my friendship, does it?

CARA

And now you have me.

MARGARET MARY

Better watch out.

CARA

At least I guess you have me. If you want me. I don't know what you want.
(MARGARET MARY *doesn't answer*)
What are you going to do?

MARGARET MARY

When?

CARA

Now. And in the future.

17

MARGARET MARY

I have no immediate plans. I've got my sights set on dinner and then—see where I am.

CARA

Would you like to have dinner together?

MARGARET MARY

No.
(She softens)
No, dear. I've already got my dinner all charted out. There's a can of Bumble Bee Tuna waiting for me on the counter.

CARA

That's not enough for dinner, not just tuna.

MARGARET MARY

It's enough for me. I'll augment it with a piece of toast, I suppose. And if I'm feeling particularly giddy I may throw in half a peach, I'll see.

CARA

That seems like a parsimonious diet. Is it from a magazine?

MARGARET MARY
(Sitting at the piano)
No, it's from necessity. I call it my inflation-deflation diet. When the cost of living goes up, my weight goes down correspondingly. According to an economic prediction I read in the *New York Times*, by 1988 I should weigh seven pounds.

CARA

Do you really have money problems?

18

MARGARET MARY

I have more money problems than I have money.

CARA

You should let me cook for you sometime.

MARGARET MARY

Sometime I will, dear.
(She plays a scale, very well indeed)

CARA

I hate to eat alone. It makes me nervous.

MARGARET MARY

Did you want to play today or—?

CARA

Oh, yes.
(She gathers up her violin as MARGARET MARY
plays another scale)
Thank God we have music.

MARGARET MARY

What did you say?

CARA

I said I'm so glad we have our waltzes to keep our friendship going.

MARGARET MARY

Yes, we owe it all to Johann Strauss and his family.
(She stares at the music books)
Ah, "Du und Du." Have you been practicing it?

19

CARA

Oh, yes. Uh-huh. Um, I told Ellen Diffendal about our sessions and she said she'd love to come and listen.
(MARGARET MARY *begins to play, delicately and confidently.* CARA *is caught off guard.* MARGARET MARY *stops*)

MARGARET MARY

Where were you? You missed the boat.

CARA

I'm sorry. I didn't know you were beginning there.

MARGARET MARY

That was the beginning of the piece, where else would I begin?

CARA

I was confused.

MARGARET MARY

Ready?
(*She begins again. She nods as* CARA *comes in smartly. They play smoothly enough for a stretch until* CARA *wanders off. She stops, flustered.* MARGARET MARY *stops*)

CARA

I'm sorry.

MARGARET MARY

It doesn't matter, I'm sure Mr. Strauss had his problems with it, too.
(*She smiles at* CARA *and waits*)

CARA

What about Ellen Diffendal? She's the one on the walker, you know. Polio victim. Could she come and listen sometime?

MARGARET MARY

No. I'm not interested in giving recitals. Not even to polio victims.

CARA

(An outburst)

You're such a maverick.

MARGARET MARY

Such a what?

CARA

A *maverick*. So independent. All the ladies in the lobby talk about you, ask me questions. I don't know what to say. They think you don't like them.

MARGARET MARY

Damned perceptive of them.

CARA

I thought the same myself when you and Mrs. Delalagro used to *parade* through, so indifferent, having so much fun. I couldn't have been more surprised when you came up to me at the elevator.

MARGARET MARY

It was your violin. It struck a sentimental chord.

CARA

I was glad you did. I like being your friend. You should come and sit with us sometime.

MARGARET MARY

You must be mad. I wouldn't be caught dead sitting in the lobby with those characters, staring at everybody, chattering away to the ninny beside you, or to yourself. They look like ugly teenage girls at a costume dance, yapping as loud as they can so they won't have to realize how alone they are. Not a trace of pride or dignity. I detest those ladies, the *bitches*.

CARA
(Shocked)

Is that so? Well, when you insult them, you insult me, and I don't have to be insulted by anyone. I do not. I draw my lines. I was going to invite you to a meeting of the tenants' association, I was going to *include* you, and ask you to make sandwiches, but you don't want to do anything like that.

MARGARET MARY

No. No, I'm afraid I couldn't make too many sandwiches. I only have the one can of Bumble Bee. And it's the small size.

CARA

I know what you're doing, you're making fun of me. Well, I *do* have my pride, and I *do* have *dignity,* and I have other things to do. There *are* those in this building who appreciate me, and who like me. *I* can *go*.

MARGARET MARY

Fine. Good. Go. Do as you wish.

22

CARA

I'm going to go.
>(*She steps back, looks at the violin case, can't
decide what to do*)
Mr. Roberton in 913 has asked me to walk his standard
poodles for him. What do you think of that?

MARGARET MARY

I think you'd better take a large pooper scooper.
>(CARA *glares at* MARGARET MARY, *storms to the
door and exits.* MARGARET MARY *sits still, she
stares off into space. She puts her hand to her face.
After a moment, the entrance door opens and* CARA
enters. Seeing MARGARET MARY *looking so morose,
she steps quietly into the room*)

CARA

Hello.

MARGARET MARY

You've come crawling back, have you?

CARA

Do you want to be friends? I mean, what do you want?

MARGARET MARY

I want to go to Iowa.

CARA

What?

MARGARET MARY

I thought it might be nice to go back to Iowa, where I
haven't been for . . . twenty-two years. My sister, you know
has nine grandchildren.

23

CARA

I didn't know that. I didn't know you were thinking about going to Iowa. I didn't even know you were from Iowa. To live, you mean?

MARGARET MARY

I'm not sure Iowa even exists. You never hear about it.

CARA

Would you do it soon? I mean, you wouldn't give up this beautiful apartment, would you? And your furniture and everything?

MARGARET MARY

Hmm? Who knows? Are we going to try the Strauss again? Or would it set you off on another tangent? Ready?
(She begins to play. CARA *comes in smoothly and* MARGARET MARY *nods at her. They play a stretch until* MARGARET MARY *botches it up this time. She stops, alarmed.* CARA *stops)*
Well, it's contagious, whatever it is.

CARA

You just made a little boo-boo, that's all. Anyone can.

MARGARET MARY

If I lose my fingers, that will be that.
*(*MARGARET MARY *stares at her hands.* CARA *stands by her, uncomfortable. A moment passes)*

CARA
(Carefully)
You know, if you're really having trouble with money, I could move in here with you, and share the rent and the expenses.

24

MARGARET MARY

No thanks.

CARA

I could cook and clean for you, and we could have wild times. My floral divan would look so cute in this room.

MARGARET MARY

I'm sure it looks cute right where it is.

CARA

Aren't you cool? How you do it, I don't know. Well, it's not normal, is it? Living alone. Human beings aren't meant to be alone. Don't you get lonely? I do. You don't think I get lonely down there in 204?

MARGARET MARY

I doubt it. You're rarely in 204. Besides you're the belle of the building, everybody loves you.

CARA

Except you.

MARGARET MARY

I'm a maverick.

CARA

Why can't I move in?

MARGARET MARY

Oh, bother, you practically have moved in. You come and go, you eat bonbons as fast as I put them out.

CARA

Haven't you heard that two heads are better than one?

MARGARET MARY

Even if one is a cabbage is the way that goes, I believe. I'm familiar with the philosophy, but I don't subscribe to it.

CARA

(Fighting back)

Well, you were buddy-buddy enough with Mrs. Delalagro.

MARGARET MARY

Be careful, Cara. You're walking on mucky ground. Mrs. Delalagro kept her head in her own apartment and she had no kitty making messes under the beds.

CARA

What? Ralphie never makes messes.

MARGARET MARY

Then he's an amazing cat.

CARA

If you'd ever come to my apartment you'd see. He confines himself to his kitty litter.

MARGARET MARY

I don't like kitty litter and I don't like kitties. They both smell.

(She has picked up a cushion, which she sets on the bench, and lowers herself onto it. CARA tries to help but MARGARET MARY waves her away)

CARA

Why won't you let anyone help you?

MARGARET MARY
(Strongly)

I *don't need help.* I *enjoy* my freedom. I enjoy my indepen-
dence. And I enjoy my loneliness. I enjoy walking *alone* to
Gristedes and checking my empty mailbox *alone.* Do you
understand? I don't *need.* Period.

(She glares at CARA, *who looks at her without
comment. She calms a bit)*

I gave you a key because I can't hear the bell, and I don't
always hear a knock. It didn't mean I wanted to go steady.

(Then brightly)

Come on, let's play, dear, shall we? We'll pick it up where
I dropped it.

*(*CARA *peers at the music)*

You don't have to hang over me like that, do you? Ready?

*(*CARA *backs up a step or two. Again* MARGARET
MARY *nods and smiles. The playing sparkles)*

Now we're cooking.

(The music continues)

Scene Two

"Gelaufigkeit" by Carl Czerny

Spring. Afternoon.

The piece has continued between the scenes. The music has moved in spurts. The piano has raced ahead. The violin has faltered, then sprinted past. They have moved in opposite directions. The piano has stopped to wait. When the violin has botched a stretch, the piano has repeated it, louder, and again, louder still. The violin has tried it, botched it again, tried it a third time, almost gotten it. They've played it together. It's been a lively conversation, or an argument.

Now the playing is high-speed and hot, with nary a blunder heard. MARGARET MARY *is wearing a light skirt and sweater, and* CARA, *a different colorful dress. She is doing her playing from the middle of the room, some six or eight feet from the piano. A window is open and the day is bright. The ladies zip into their finish, a glorious, harmonious crescendo, not too far, probably, from*

29

what Mr. Strauss had in mind. They stop, trium-
phant and pleased.

MARGARET MARY

It's a shame Ed Sullivan couldn't have lived.

CARA

We were really crackling, weren't we?

MARGARET MARY

At a fever pitch. Have a bonbon, Cara.
(She reaches behind the piano for a cane and
pulls herself up with difficulty)

CARA

Thank you.
(She pops one into her mouth)
Mmmm.
(She eyes the bowl)

MARGARET MARY

Just one.

CARA

What are you doing?

MARGARET MARY

Walking. Or at least trying to.
(She moves slowly away from the piano, then stops
and leans on the cane as she reaches for her toes)

CARA

Did you read what it said about Elizabeth Taylor in the
Post?

MARGARET MARY
(Closing the subject)

No!

CARA

What are you doing now?

MARGARET MARY

My toe-touching exercises. It's interesting that even though I seem to get smaller all the time, my toes seem to get further away.

CARA

I tried exercising once. It's not that much fun really.
(She watches uncomfortably)
I wish you could have come to the meeting last night in the laundry room. Big stuff. We went until ten-thirty.
(She pauses)
You'll never guess what.
(MARGARET MARY doesn't even try)
I was nominated to be floor rep.
(Again there is no response)
I couldn't believe it. I've never been nominated for anything. Apparently people do like me. I declined. You're allowed to do that. I said I had other priorities. I said other things came first, like friendship and loyalty. And there will be time enough for glory and service. So it went to Jeffrey Roosevelt, in 210, who is not related to the President Roosevelts, but is actually mulatto, I'm pretty sure.

MARGARET MARY

Did you want to play some more?
(She exercises her fingers quickly)

31

CARA

Oh, yes. I thought you'd be too tired.

MARGARET MARY

No, twenty-five toe touches don't wear me out as much as
you'd think.
(She flips through a book of music)

CARA

I've got Jell-O jelling. We can have some later.

MARGARET MARY
(Not excited)

Jell-O?

CARA

Adie Nims showed me how to mix in bananas and ice
cream. It's delish! I can go down and get it.
(Rather than answer, MARGARET MARY suddenly
plays a quick stretch of "Die Schule der Gelaufigkeit." It's a dizzying display of technique and it
leaves CARA open-mouthed)
What was that?

MARGARET MARY

What was what?

CARA

That music. It was very good.

MARGARET MARY

Thank you. That was "Die Schule der Gelaufigkeit," by
Carl Czerny.

CARA

You played it so fast.

MARGARET MARY

Yes. It's meant to be played fast. That's what the title means: The School of Velocity. *Molto Allegro.* Very fast.

CARA

Oh.

MARGARET MARY
(Opening another book)

Well! What about Rimski-Korsakov? I'm in a Korsakov sort of mood. You've been practicing this, haven't you?

CARA

Oh, God.

MARGARET MARY

Hmm? "The Flight of the Bumblebee." Shall we buzz through it?
(She smiles, feeling good. She plunges in with vigor. CARA stands petrified. She inches toward the piano, squinting at the music. MARGARET MARY stops)
You've missed the boat. I'll come back for you.
(She plays the beginning again. CARA sneaks closer to the piano, listens hard for her cue, misses it, and is just lifting violin to chin when MARGARET MARY stops. CARA shrugs and smiles sheepishly. She giggles. MARGARET MARY smiles . . . stops again)

33

CARA

We're having fun, aren't we?

MARGARET MARY

At Mr. Korsakov's expense, yes.
   *(She prepares to start once more just as the door-
   bell rings.* CARA *turns to look)*
Giving up?

CARA

The doorbell rang.

MARGARET MARY

Did it? Well, go answer it. How exciting. I hope you've
saved some bonbons.
   *(*CARA *opens the door and* ROBIN *enters. She is
   pretty, blondish, shortish, thirtyish, at once enthusiastic and jaded. She speaks with a powerful
   Brooklyn accent, her clothes are on the outrageous
   side of fashionable, and her hair is a sight. She
   nods at* CARA*)*

ROBIN

Hiya.
            (To MARGARET MARY*)*
Hiya.

MARGARET MARY
            (Staring at ROBIN*)*
Who are you?

ROBIN

My name is Robin Bird.
            *(*CARA *loves this. She roars with laughter)*

34

MARGARET MARY

What are you cackling about?

CARA

She said her name is *Robin Bird.*
                    (She laughs)

MARGARET MARY

I see. That *is* interesting, but I don't believe it warrants
rudeness.
                    (To ROBIN*)*
Sounds like you made that up.

ROBIN

I did.

MARGARET MARY

What was your name before?

ROBIN

Roseanne Mazzarrella.

CARA

That's Italian.

ROBIN

I know.

MARGARET MARY

I'd think you've done a wise thing. My name is Margaret
Mary Elderdice, which I didn't make up, and this is my
neighbor, Cara Varnum. How may we help you, Miss
Bird?

ROBIN

I'm here about the job.

MARGARET MARY

The job?

CARA

There are no jobs here.

ROBIN

*(She fishes in her pocket and pulls out an index
card. She reads)*
"Wanted. Someone to live in. Free room and board, light
housekeeping, companionship, arrangements to be negotiated."

CARA

What? You're in the wrong place. Let me see that.
*(ROBIN hands the card to CARA, who reads it
quickly. MARGARET MARY looks with great interest
at ROBIN, who smiles at her nervously)*
Where did you get this?

ROBIN

On the board at the Rainbow Bookstore on Broadway.

CARA

The Rainbow Bookstore. They've got dirty books in there.
*(She is quite stunned. She turns to MARGARET
MARY)*
Did you write this?

MARGARET MARY

Yes.

CARA

What were you doing in the Rainbow Bookstore?

MARGARET MARY

Hanging it on the board.

CARA

They've got naked people in there.

MARGARET MARY

No, they don't. I'm sure I would have noticed.

CARA

In the books. Little naked children on the covers. I've seen them. It used to be a religious bookstore, Presbyterian, I believe. I don't think it is anymore. Why do you need someone to live in?

MARGARET MARY

I just do.

CARA

I could live in for free.

MARGARET MARY

I thought it best, dear, that I look elsewhere.
(She pulls herself up and hobbles to a chair)
Sit down, Miss Bird. Beside me, so I can hear you. Sit down, Cara.
(The ladies sit, CARA apart from the others. She pouts, and MARGARET MARY stares at ROBIN)
I'm finding this utterly fascinating. But I have to ask you an impertinent question. Why would you be interested in this sort of situation? I mean, you're young and pretty and, if you'll pardon the expression, white.

37

ROBIN

You don't want to know.

MARGARET MARY

I beg your pardon?

ROBIN

It's a long story.

MARGARET MARY

Can you give us a capsule summary?

ROBIN

Um. Well, you know. I'm an actress.
*(She looks quickly for a response. All she gets is a
look at the ceiling from* CARA*)*
Although nobody else really knows that. I *intend* to be an
actress, that's my dream. Um. I'm from Brooklyn, which
you might be able to tell, although most recently I've been
living in Connecticut, which is probably why I seem a little
crazy. I've had a lot of jobs, I was married for seven years—
I hope that doesn't screw up my, you know, eligibility. I'm
not married now, I'm *un*married. But, I've had some experience in housekeeping, though I've never won any prizes
for it.
(She looks about)
This place is huge. So, anyway, somewhere along the way
my husband became gay and um . . .

MARGARET MARY

Became what?

CARA

Homo.

MARGARET MARY

Oh, oh, gay. Go on, this is good.

ROBIN

Well, anyway, when Peter Pan flew away, I counted the rooms in our house for a couple of months—there's only four rooms—and then I said, "What are you doing, dummy?" And I decided to do something incredible with my life, and I came into the city and was an incredible waitress for three months, until that made me crazy, and then my cousin, who I've known all my life, crapped out on me, and said I had to move out of her apartment 'cause I was threatening her libido, so I've been staying in this rooming house for women, which is like the ultimate answer to the all-time question: "How low can you go?" Then I was in the Rainbow Bookstore looking for something interesting to read, but they didn't have anything, and then I saw your little card, and I'm sorry I took it down. Can I use your bathroom? I figured I'd at least get to use the bathroom.

MARGARET MARY

Hmm? Oh, yes. Through the wooden door, straight back till you find it. We're not being very good hostesses, are we, Cara?

(ROBIN *heads for the door.* CARA *glowers at her*)

CARA
(Unpleasantly)

Like a bonbon?

ROBIN

No thanks.

(*She exits.* CARA *now fixes her icy stare on* MAR-GARET MARY, *who is pulling herself up*)

39

CARA
(Whispering)

You've lost your gumballs.

MARGARET MARY

I beg your pardon?

CARA
(Whispering)

You must be *nuts.*

MARGARET MARY

I can't hear a word you're saying.

CARA
(Loudly)

That's because I'm whispering.

MARGARET MARY

Whispering? You should never whisper to a deaf person, Cara. It shows a lack of good sense.

CARA
(Rising)

All right, I'll say it out then. You can't hire that girl to live in.

MARGARET MARY

Why not?

CARA

She was married to a homosexual.

MARGARET MARY

So? People hire minority groups all the time. I might as well try dipping into wives of homosexuals. That would seem to be a virtually untapped resource.

CARA

Don't you know all hired people are thieves? I thought you didn't have any money.

MARGARET MARY

That's the part that has to be negotiated. Cara, why don't you do me a huge favor and stop fretting? How about skipping down to your apartment and getting your Jell-O? Then we could have a Jell-O party and we could play for Miss Bird. She could see what a whiz you are on your violin. How about it? Hmm?

CARA

Oh, sure. It's get-rid-of-Cara time. Story of my life.
(She heads for the door)
I've got to look in on Ralphie anyway. At least he understands loyalty.
(She exits. MARGARET MARY *steps down to the piano, looking rather exuberant. She sits and begins to play the Czerny.* ROBIN *enters)*

ROBIN

That's a great bathroom. It has real character.
(She stands by the piano. MARGARET MARY *stops)*
That's pretty. You're a virtuoso, huh?

MARGARET MARY

Virtually. I'm curious about something. Didn't you have

some idea about your husband's proclivity when you first
married him?

Huh?

You didn't know he was the way he was at first?

He wasn't that way at first. It was a degenerative process.

I see. You can sit down again, unless you're planning to run
along now that you've used the facilities.
(ROBIN sits)
You know I had forgotten I put up that notice. I did it on
a whim.

You mean you don't really want anyone?

I didn't say that. I said I did it on a whim. I'm amazed to
have anyone reply. What do you think of this? Does it seem
palatable to you? Or what?

(Not understanding)
Palatable? Well, there's palatable and there's palatable,
isn't there?

I suppose so. What I was wondering was whether you'd
like living in a place like this, with a person like me.

ROBIN
(Looking about)

Well, I'd have to chew on that. Then I could tell you how palatable it was.

MARGARET MARY

That seems reasonable. You'd have your own room, kitchen privileges, I'd supply the food. It doesn't look as though you require great quantities. I couldn't pay you very much.

ROBIN

That would be okay.

MARGARET MARY

How cheaply would you work?

ROBIN

How cheap do you pay?

MARGARET MARY

Um. Fifty dollars a week.

ROBIN

Fifty dollars, fifty dollars.
(She considers it)
I could live on fifty dollars. Who needs money?

MARGARET MARY

I do, for one. This is none of my business, but don't you receive any money at all from your queer husband?

ROBIN

Nope. I did, but I don't. I refused it. It's my only revenge. He was a fruitcake long before he decided to become one.

43

MARGARET MARY

I think I know what you mean. Good husbands are a rare breed. Most of them would make better wives. I was married to an oddball myself.

ROBIN

Was he queer?

MARGARET MARY

Not in the same sense of the word.

ROBIN

Oh, he was just a flake, huh?

MARGARET MARY

That's a good word for him. A *snowflake*. That's what he was. One of a kind.
(She thinks about it, pleased with the image)
He played country music on the guitar, that sort of thing. I believe it's why I lost my hearing. You can see there's not much to be done here. Do you cook?

ROBIN

Not too well.

MARGARET MARY

It's all right, I do. Would you like a bonbon?

ROBIN

No thanks. Two of those little turkeys and it would be cellulite city.

MARGARET MARY

You know, occasionally I border on not being able to understand you. A good actress has to enunciate. E-nun-see-ate.

ROBIN

(Mildly defensive)

This is something I'm cog-ni-zant of.

MARGARET MARY

Good. Now, what about your acting career? This intrigues me very much. I take it you don't agree that the theater is dead.

ROBIN

(Surprised)

No! It better not be. That would be just my luck, wouldn't it? It can't be dead.

MARGARET MARY

Well, it's only a rumor. It was alive the last time I went. But then, too, so was Ethel Barrymore. Have you been preparing? Studying, and taking dance classes and voice classes and reading the great plays?

ROBIN

(Looking at her blankly)

No. I heard about a class. But you have to audition, so I'm taking my time. I don't want to scare anybody. Including myself.

MARGARET MARY

That sounds very wise. You remind me of myself with my piano, back at the turn of the century. I was far and away the best pianist in Oskaloosa, Iowa. So naturally I came to New York, dizzy with excitement. And paralyzed with fear. I got my toes wet gradually, studying with a great master. And then, unfortunately, I lost track of my purposes and put my shoes back on. And then I met Happy Harry Eld-

45

erdice, and *that* was *that*. I spent the next thirty-seven years playing for him. We laughed a great deal. It was a brilliant marriage. Flawed, but brilliant.

> (MARGARET MARY *is lost in her story for a moment.* ROBIN *smiles at her*)

ROBIN

Well, you sure play beautiful.

MARGARET MARY

Do you think so? Aren't you sweet? My piano, which I've had for forty-one years, is like an old horse. Fortunately it knows the way home. It used to support me. I had a number of very fine students at one point, but I don't now. Musicians seem to be put off when the instructor is hard of hearing.

> *(She pauses)*

Now I am left to provide entertainment for the walls and the rats and roaches.

ROBIN
> *(She looks around uncomfortably)*

What about your friend?

MARGARET MARY

My friend? You mean Cara? Cara would like to be my friend. She's rather like a cumulus cloud: very nice but she blocks the sun, if you know what I mean.

ROBIN
> *(Not really sure)*

Uh huh.

46

MARGARET MARY

Mrs. Delalagro was my friend. She played the oboe, she read books and had ideas. Together we made the most beautiful music this side of the Met. She killed herself.

ROBIN

Why?

MARGARET MARY

Because she's a fool! Because her rent went up and Con Ed went up and the telephone went up, and her savings went down and her spirits went down. I won't forgive her this one.

(She stands still. Upset)

ROBIN

I'm sorry.

MARGARET MARY
(Snapping out of it)
Do you like music? Or are you a rock-and-roll aficionado?

ROBIN

I have diverse tastes. I like music.

MARGARET MARY

It's a wonderful tonic, isn't it?
(Pause)
You don't drink, do you?

ROBIN

Nah.

MARGARET MARY

Take drugs?

ROBIN

Not really.

MARGARET MARY
(Pause)
You don't play the oboe, do you?

ROBIN

Oboe? Oh, no.

MARGARET MARY

Pity. Very few people do play the oboe. It's a lonely instrument. You don't play the guitar, do you?

ROBIN

I took one lesson.

MARGARET MARY

One lesson. How did it go?

ROBIN

Not bad.

MARGARET MARY

Why did you quit at one? Did you feel you'd absorbed
everything you needed to know about the guitar?

ROBIN

No, it was my teacher. He tried to feel me up.

MARGARET MARY

Feel you up? How extraordinary. Was this early in the lesson? Or near the end?

ROBIN

He'd taught me the C chord and G-7, and he was showing me E minor.

MARGARET MARY

Ah, those minor chords. They seem to set off something in people. What about dating? Would you be planning on bringing in the New York Rangers or something?

ROBIN

No, I'm off dating. Too much trouble. Let 'em suffer for a while.
(MARGARET MARY *smiles*)
I mean basically it all sucks anyway.

MARGARET MARY

I beg your pardon?

ROBIN

Relationships. It doesn't matter, it's just sort of confusing, that's all. I mean life is not your basic seventeenth-century novel. Everything is not black and white. Now we're talking colors all the time, we're talking shades.

MARGARET MARY

Have you read a lot of seventeenth-century novels?

ROBIN

I've read enough of them. I was reading in *Time* magazine, or *Vogue,* one of those, that three out of every four mar-

49

riages are going to fail. You know? I mean, wow, I'd rather buy gold. At least if its value goes down four hundred bucks you still have a handful of gold. You know what I'm saying?

MARGARET MARY
(Thinking about it)

No. I don't have a clue.

ROBIN

I'm talking relationships, man-woman, connections-disconnections, sexual communication. You know. Dirty stuff.

MARGARET MARY

Oh. Well. *I* think there's a great moral imbalance in this country, if that's what you're talking about.

ROBIN

Um . . . yeah.

MARGARET MARY

And by that I don't mean sin or anything that exciting. What depresses me is the decay of moral fiber. Not enough good people. All the true sensitivities are flung out the window. I'm sick of people who only play at living, who try to con life and hide from it and give it no respect.

ROBIN

You're right. Most people suck.
(MARGARET MARY smiles, she laughs)

MARGARET MARY

Are you a good person?

50

ROBIN

Definitely. No question about it.

MARGARET MARY
(She smiles)

I find you very amusing.

ROBIN

That's nice.

MARGARET MARY

Very sharp. What I would be paying you for, Robin, would be companionship. That's the key word. I don't meet many people. I'm a maverick. I need someone to talk to, I need conversation. Not twenty-four hours a day, just sometimes. And I'm willing to pay for it. I find it most encouraging to think that fifty dollars a week conceivably can get me conversation in English. I was prepared to learn Vietnamese.
(Pause)
How would you feel about walking out in public with an old invalid?

ROBIN

Fine. I love to walk.

MARGARET MARY

How would you feel about walking slowly? Do you have a mother and father back in Bedford Stuyvesant or somewhere whose permission you would need to live here?

ROBIN

I've got a mother and father, but they gave up a long time ago. Actually they would find this very Catholic.

MARGARET MARY
(Enthusiastically)
I think it would be a lot of fun, don't you?

ROBIN
I don't know.

MARGARET MARY
I see.

ROBIN
I tell you what I'm going to do. I'm going to chew on it.
You know? I'm not sure how much I'm equipped to handle.

MARGARET MARY
(Touchily)
I see. Well, fine, as you wish. Take your time.

ROBIN
Your doorbell's ringing.

MARGARET MARY
Is it? What a busy day. Could you answer it? Let's see how
you do with something like that.

ROBIN
(Heading for the door)
I think I can handle opening the door.
(She does, and in walks SERGE, *all aglow)*

SERGE
Ah, ha ha, you have found 1506, you are so smart.

ROBIN

Yip.

(She closes the door as SERGE *walks to* MARGARET MARY*)*

SERGE

Miss Elderdice, hello. I have this key for you door, that you wanted. Was very uneasy making.

MARGARET MARY

Thank you, Serge. Once again you've come through with aplomb.

SERGE

Thank you.

MARGARET MARY

What do I owe you for your diligence?

SERGE

What? No money. Is my pleasure.

MARGARET MARY

Well, bless your heart. This is my friend, Robin Bird.

SERGE

This is something I know. So beautiful I could die.
(He gazes at her. The entrance door opens and CARA *bounds in, carrying a large bowl of Jell-O)*

CARA
(With great to-do)

I brought the Jell-O.

MARGARET MARY

Oh, good. Do you like Jell-O, Robin?

ROBIN

No.

MARGARET MARY

Serge?

SERGE

Jell-O? No.
(He shakes his head)

CARA
(Firmly)
You'll like this Jell-O. It's not jelled yet. I'm putting it in
your fridge, Margaret Mary.
(Petulantly)
If it's all right.
(She exits into the kitchen)

MARGARET MARY

How splendid. Sit down, Robin, and Cara and I will per-
form for you while you mull over your decision. And while
the Jell-O jells. Sit down, Serge.
*(ROBIN sits on the sofa, delicately resting one foot
on the coffee table. SERGE is quick to sit beside her,
leaning toward her and smiling. She subtly leans
away. CARA marches in)*
Come on, Cara. We're going to play our Korsakov for our
guests.

CARA
(Looking suddenly ill)

Oh, God!
(She barks at ROBIN)

Get your feet off the table!

ROBIN
(Putting her feet down)

Why are you so hostile?

CARA

Hostile? Hostile?
(She gathers up her violin)

MARGARET MARY

Is the Korsakov all right, or would you prefer something
else?

CARA

The Korsakov.
(She lifts her violin defiantly)

Of course.

MARGARET MARY

Good. That's the spirit. Ready?
(She begins to play with gusto. CARA *very nearly
misses her cue, overconcentrating as she is, but in
she plunges. She plays with rare determination,
almost perfectly.* SERGE *smiles at* ROBIN)

SERGE
(To ROBIN)

Is so beautiful.

*(*ROBIN *looks at him and nods)*
My wonderful friends. You want to dance?
> *(*ROBIN *shakes her head.* MARGARET MARY *looks*
> *back at her and smiles.* ROBIN *smiles, then glances*
> *at* CARA, *who scowls at her.* SERGE *smiles at* ROBIN,
> *then at* CARA. *The music dips and twists, and* CARA
> *and* MARGARET MARY *give it a fine go)*

MARGARET MARY
(Jubilantly)
Now we're cooking!
> *(The music continues)*

SCENE THREE

"PLAYING TOGETHER IS FUN" BY SAUL MINSCH AND WOLFGANG MOZART

Summer. Morning.

The piece has continued. The piano has faded and the violin has frolicked along in its jumpy fashion. It has left "The Flight of the Bumblebee," given the tricky stretches of "Du und Du" an unsuccessful try, and is now cavorting through "My Hero," very smugly.

CARA is sitting on the piano bench. She wears another bright dress, and she perspires as she plays. Behind her, SERGE is poking at the air conditioner, frowning and sweating. He wears a short-sleeved workshirt. He looks at CARA and smiles fondly.

The room seems a bit less sparkly. There are magazine piles and other clutter, and the furniture is off-kilter. The sun pours in the window.

CARA *finishes the piece with a whimper, and sets down her violin. She dabs at her face with a hanky.* SERGE *realizes she's finished and he claps appreciatively.* CARA *waves him off, irritated.*

CARA

I hate summer. It's worse than winter.
> *(She looks about the room, shakes her head)*

This room has lost its luster. Something's wrong with this room.

SERGE
(Looking about)

Is okay.

CARA

Margaret Mary has lost her luster, too. Have you noticed that? She's lost her gumballs, I think.
> *(SERGE looks at her without comment. He steps to the mirrored door)*

What are you doing?

SERGE

Checking wires.

CARA

There are rats in that room. This is their time of year, you know. They go crazy in the summer.

SERGE

Mrs. Varnum, there is no rats in this room. One time you had one little baby rat, and now always I have filled the little baby hole and put in the poison and the traps. Is no rat would dare come in this room.
> *(SERGE shrugs and opens the door)*

CARA

Be careful! I would *die* if I got bitten by a rat and got the bubonic plague or something.

(SERGE *shakes his head. He steps into the rat room, closes the door. Suddenly he screams)*

SERGE
(Offstage)

Acch! Acch! Is giant rats everywhere! Help me, God! Acch!

(*He bangs something.* CARA *jumps up, terrified, ready to run.* SERGE *opens the door and smiles mischievously)*

I was making joke.

(CARA *glares at him)*

I am so sorry. Is very funny.

(*He smiles sheepishly and disappears into the room, closing the door.* CARA *stares after him, looks about with distaste. The entrance door opens and* MARGARET MARY *enters. She walks with two canes. She has the* New York Times *tucked under an arm and she smiles when she sees* CARA*)*

MARGARET MARY

Hello, pumpkin.

(*She moves slowly but with gusto)*

CARA

Hi, Margaret Mary. Been for a walk?

MARGARET MARY
(With good-natured sarcasm)

No, I was roller-skating, dear.

(*She flings the paper onto the table)*

It's a crystal day. Enough blue sky to make a Dutchman's

59

britches. Riverside Park's full to the brim. You should get out. I saw all your friends on the benches, cackling away.

CARA

Too hot. I get bumps.

MARGARET MARY

I beg your pardon?

CARA
(Snapping)
Prickly heat! I get rashes, *rashes!*

MARGARET MARY

You're in a vexy sort of mood, aren't you?

CARA

You wouldn't understand.
(The doorbell rings. CARA looks at MARGARET MARY, then goes and opens the door. In steps ROBIN, wearing baggy pants and a flimsy halter. She carries several letters)

ROBIN

Hiya. I forgot my key.

CARA

Oh, for God's sake.

MARGARET MARY

Oh, you got the mail. How'd we do?

ROBIN

Not too great. An application for an American Express

60

card, a letter from our congressman and a postcard from my ex-husband. Junk mail.

(She tears up the mail and drops it into a waste-basket. CARA watches and rolls her eyes to the ceiling. There is a loud bang behind the mirrored door)

Acch!

(She jumps back. MARGARET MARY holds up a cane. CARA had forgotten SERGE and she moves away. The door opens and SERGE comes out smiling)

SERGE

Hello, Robin Bird.

ROBIN

You scared me.

SERGE
(He studies ROBIN)
You are so beautiful could break my heart.

ROBIN

Thank you.

SERGE

Hello, Miss Elderdice. So good to see you.

MARGARET MARY

Thank you, Serge. Any luck with the air conditioner?

SERGE
(Crossing to the window)
This air conditioner? You know why this does not work? Is no good, that's why.

61

MARGARET MARY
Can you fix it?

SERGE
I don't know. Not today. Is too hot. I going now. Good-bye.
(He bows)

MARGARET MARY
Good-bye, dear. Do try to come fix the thing before we all
perish from the heat, won't you?

SERGE
(Snapping testily)
Yes! Okay!
(He calms down)
For you, my friends, I will. When is cooler.
(He turns, stops by ROBIN*)*
So beautiful. Many times I think, "What does Robin Bird
look like with no clothes?" Hah! My wife, you know, I tell
her, "Get thin, don't be so fat. Buy some nice swimming
suits like these Americans."
(He shakes his head)
Is impossible. Bigger every day. *Impossible.* In New York
in the summertime I die. I look at you, I want to die. This
is life. Good-bye.
(He exits)

MARGARET MARY
I like him better in the *winter,* odoriferously speaking.

ROBIN
He's sweet.

CARA
He's a moron.

MARGARET MARY

He's a sweet moron. I think we should have some iced tea. What do you say? Robin?

ROBIN

Great.

> *(She doesn't move. She is now leaning over the coffee table, studying the paper.* CARA *stares at her as* MARGARET MARY *works her way up to the kitchen)*

MARGARET MARY

Cara? Iced tea?

CARA

Yes. *Please.*

> *(*MARGARET MARY *exits)*

You could have got it for her. That's what I'd do if I was living here. I'd get things for her.

ROBIN

She likes to get things for herself. You know?

> *(She returns to the paper)*

Why do you suppose the *New York Times* has no funny papers?

CARA

No sense of humor. I like the *Post* myself. It's got style.

> *(She stares at* ROBIN*)*

You do have nice boobies.

ROBIN

> *(Surprised)*

Oh. Thank you, Cara.

CARA

You should wear a bra though. I always wear a bra myself. Do you know how many women have mastectomies *every day?*

ROBIN

One thousand?

CARA

Ten thousand. *Ten thousand.*

ROBIN

Where do you get these little statistics from?

CARA

I get 'em.
(MARGARET MARY enters, balancing in one hand a tray with a pitcher of tea and three glasses, and leaning on her canes with the other)

MARGARET MARY

Here we are.
(She arrives at the coffee table)
Move the paper, dear. They don't mention Iowa in there, do they?

ROBIN
(Gathering up the paper)
No, but there's an article I want to save about pigeons. I never knew there were so many kinds of pigeons.

MARGARET MARY
(She pours the tea)
There's only one kind of pigeon: filthy. I don't understand why people delight in feeding them all the time. They must

be the most overfed bird in the world. You'll have to come over, Cara, we don't deliver.

(CARA *steps over and they all sit*)

Did Robin tell you about our adventures?

CARA
(Unpleasantly)

No.

MARGARET MARY

We had a *ducky* time. First we ran into my friend, the derelict. She was dancing in the street, enjoying herself no end. She dances quite well, too. Robin went right up to her and said hello. I tried that once when I found her lying in front of the movie theater. And she greeted me with the most remarkable string of profanity. She likes Robin though. What did she tell you her name was?

ROBIN

Mr. Goo.

MARGARET MARY

Mr.—Goo. What a glorious name. How do you suppose she got like that anyway?

CARA

Poor diet.

MARGARET MARY

Is that it?

ROBIN

It's New York. Everybody's crazy in New York. All you've got to do is let go for two minutes and you'll find yourself dancing in the street and wetting your pants on the bus.

(The ladies contemplate this as they sip their drinks)

Everybody's crazy, and everybody's horny. New York's the horniest city in the world.

MARGARET MARY

All the men were staring at Robin.

ROBIN

They weren't staring at me.

MARGARET MARY

Well, they weren't staring at *me,* dear.

CARA

They would if you wore a pornographic top like that.

MARGARET MARY

I imagine they would, yes.

ROBIN

I don't need men looking at me. I don't look at them.

CARA

Then you should put your clothes on.

ROBIN
(Strongly)

No. They should grow up.

MARGARET MARY

One gentleman got a little fresh with Robin.

ROBIN

I wouldn't call that getting fresh. Men don't get fresh anymore, it's passé.

CARA

What did he do?

ROBIN

He opened up the barn door and let out the pony.

CARA
(It takes a moment to register)
What? He did that? And you saw it?

ROBIN

Actually he aimed it at Margaret Mary. She had the better view.

CARA

That's disgusting.

MARGARET MARY

It wasn't disgusting really. Not as those things go.

CARA

Did you call a policeman?

MARGARET MARY

He *was* a policeman, wasn't he, Robin? He had on a uniform.

ROBIN

He was a security guard.

CARA

He could have raped you!

MARGARET MARY

No, he wasn't a rapist. That's not what he was about at all.
Not judging by his rapier anyway.

CARA

What do you mean?

MARGARET MARY

His. . . . It was not ready for battle. It was at peace.

CARA

I'm not sure I know what you're talking about.

MARGARET MARY

Then I don't think I should tell you. He just wanted attention. And we gave him ours briefly.

CARA

You should come to a meeting of the West Side Women's
Association sometime. That's the sort of thing they love to
hear about.

MARGARET MARY

I bet.

ROBIN

Have you ever had sex, Cara?

CARA

Otherwise the park was about normal, was it?

MARGARET MARY

Oh, yes. More babies than I've ever seen. It *was* an early winter, wasn't it?

CARA

I don't know where they all come from.
(She looks quickly at ROBIN*)*
I mean, I *know* where they come from, I just don't understand why women want them.

MARGARET MARY

Babies, babies, babies. I wanted a baby once.
(To CARA*, joking)*
It's too late now. I just thought it was part of being a woman, part of the experience. A little extra feature that makes us superior to men.

CARA

I think there's far too much emphasis put on experiences. Every time you turn around it's sex or it's abortions or women's lib or homosexuality or orgasms. What ever happened to just living?

ROBIN

It died out.

CARA

I suppose you're the great authority on living, aren't you? Well, I've lived too, Miss Mazzarrella. It's true I didn't marry, and that was selfish of me, I know. I've been a good girl all my life, but that doesn't mean I haven't lived. You don't have to roll in the mud to be a pig, you know.
(She glares at ROBIN*)*

MARGARET MARY

What are you going on about?

CARA

Your roommate. She thinks she's big cheese because she's had a few affairs. I think anybody who's had sex with a lot of different men is a degenerate and should be ashamed.

MARGARET MARY

What do you call a lot?

CARA

I've never even had my period. What do you think of that?

MARGARET MARY

I think the Museum of Natural History might be interested in you.

ROBIN

Maybe you've been pregnant all these years.

CARA

Oh, ha, ha. My gynecologist says I'm a fine specimen of womanhood. And he's seen them all, believe me.

ROBIN

I could tell you gynecologist stories that would blow you away.

MARGARET MARY

I think it would be best if you didn't.

CARA

(To ROBIN, *strongly)*

Is nothing sacred? You know what we need in this world?
A return to normalcy.

ROBIN

It's too late. We've gone too far.

CARA

It's not too late for *you* to pull *your*self together. How old
are you?

ROBIN

Around thirty.

CARA

Around thirty. I like that. I'm *around* fifty myself.

MARGARET MARY

I'm around seventy.

CARA

Well, my goodness, that's interesting, isn't it? Thirty, fifty,
seventy. What do you think that means?

MARGARET MARY

It means we're all liars.

CARA

No. I never realized this before. It's really interesting.
We're each at a key age of life. Thirty, fifty, seventy.

MARGARET MARY

All we need is a ten-year-old and we can start a club.

CARA

No, really, look at us. Three gals on their own. Independent
of men. Left alone by death or by choice or by ... strange
circumstance. Three sharp cookies, each doing their own
thing. Three losers.
(ROBIN *and* MARGARET MARY *look at* CARA, *then
at each other.* ROBIN *stands*)

MARGARET MARY

Have you got something planned for today, Robin?

ROBIN

I'm going to the movies. You want to come?
(She gathers up the newspaper)

MARGARET MARY

No thanks.

ROBIN

On the East Side. It's only two dollars if you get there by
one o'clock.

MARGARET MARY

That makes it tempting, but I'm afraid I deplore movies.
They're too much like life.

CARA
(Pleasantly)
I haven't been to a movie in years.

72

ROBIN

I think I'll put on a shirt just in case I fall asleep in the theater.

(She starts for the door with the paper)

MARGARET MARY

Have you worked on your audition today?

ROBIN

Um. Yip. A little.

MARGARET MARY

Better stay and go over it a few times.

(To CARA*)*

She has her audition in two weeks for acting class. She's gotten very good at it. Want to hear it?

CARA

No.

MARGARET MARY

Robin, do it for Cara. Be good practice.

ROBIN

Nah. I've got to get going or it'll be past one.

CARA

What bus are you taking?

ROBIN

I'm going to *walk*. Through the *park*. Okay?

CARA

Okay. Big deal.

73

MARGARET MARY

If you don't work on your piece, you'll fail it, and then where will you be?

ROBIN

I'm not going to *fail it,* don't worry about it.
(To CARA)
If I take a bus I have to pay seventy-five cents each way and then the movie won't be two dollars, will it?

MARGARET MARY

You have to work, dear. You have to *work* for it.

ROBIN
(Getting angry)

I'll work on it later. I figure going to the movies is part of my training. I study the craft, you know?

MARGARET MARY

Hogwash. Do you think I became a minor musical genius by listening to the radio?

ROBIN
(Yelling)

Hey! Give me a *break,* would you? I've got my shit together! Jeez-uzz Christ! I know what I'm doing.

MARGARET MARY
(Stunned by this outburst)

I merely wished to point out that if you want something in life you have to go out and get it, it's not going to fall in your lap.

ROBIN
(Still incensed)

I guess I already know that. What do you think I am—
stupid?

> (She marches out, slamming the hall door. CARA
> turns to MARGARET MARY, a superior smile)

CARA

I'll say.

MARGARET MARY

What is it, Cara?

CARA

I was answering her question. I'll say she's stupid.

MARGARET MARY

No, she's not. She's just like Mrs. Delalagro. Vexy, vexy,
vexy.

> (She smiles fondly, and moves to the piano. CARA
> watches, feeling a bit put out)

CARA

Guess what. I'm moving.

MARGARET MARY

What did you say?

CARA

I'm moving to 1703 with Adie Nims. She's asked me.

MARGARET MARY

Well, how nice.

CARA

Yes, it is. Adie is very nice, if you can get past her religious problems. I've never had much truck for the Mormons, although I'm sure I admire what they did with the grasshoppers in Salt Lake City. I don't need such a big place all by myself. Plus, I'll be nearer to you, Margaret Mary, if you need me.

MARGARET MARY
(Sitting at the piano)
Well, I think it's wonderful.

CARA

Oh, yes, it's the best thing. My floral divan will look so cute in her living room. And she doesn't mind the cat at all, that's what she said.

MARGARET MARY
Good.
(ROBIN marches in, still irritated. She wears a lovely silk blouse. She plunks her shoulder bag on the chair and noisily rummages in it. MARGARET MARY and CARA look at her uncomfortably)
Well, don't you look pretty?

ROBIN
Thanks.

MARGARET MARY
That's a lovely blouse.

ROBIN
It's yours.

MARGARET MARY

Oh? Well, we both have good taste then, haven't we? You should tuck it in though, it would look better.

> (ROBIN *stares at her, not likely to yield.* MARGARET MARY *shrugs*)

Or, you could wear it like that. Either way.

> (ROBIN *hesitates, then tucks the blouse in. She looks at the others sheepishly*)

ROBIN

Hot weather really makes people irritable, you know what I'm saying?

MARGARET MARY

Yes.

CARA
(Trying to be sympathetic)

Oh, sure.

ROBIN

Um. I guess I could do the audition thing now. If you want me to.

CARA

I don't mind listening to it.

MARGARET MARY

No. Later, dear. When it's cooler. Robin, come and show Cara what you can do on the guitar.

> (ROBIN *shrugs, then picks up the guitar and sits on the ottoman*)

Come on. We'll show her what we've done to dear Mr.
Mozart.

(To CARA*)*

She really has extraordinary potential. Ready?

*(*MARGARET MARY *begins to play "Playing
Together Is Fun," which is actually "Twinkle,
Twinkle Little Star." On the fourth bar, she nods
at* ROBIN, *who plays a chord. A few more bars,
another chord. And so they move, choppily, but
with a certain flair.* MARGARET MARY *smiles at*
CARA, *who is not impressed. But she steps to the
piano and joins in.* MARGARET MARY *continues to
nod at* ROBIN *when it is her turn, and* CARA *does
her best to match them. After a moment, they all
achieve a sort of charming rhythm, even if the
music is repetitious and not particularly challenging.* MARGARET MARY *begins doing variations, still
nodding at* ROBIN. CARA *catches on, and does her
own variations.* MARGARET MARY *smiles at* ROBIN,
who smiles back. CARA*'s face is all determination)*

Now we're cooking.

(The music continues)

CURTAIN

INTERLUDE

"Playing Together Is Fun" by Saul
Minsch and Wolfgang Mozart"
PIANO, VIOLIN, GUITAR
(Being a demonstration of basic skills, teamwork, and interplay,
and the hazards and thrills included therein. The playing is sim-
ple, silly, creative, and strange.)

"Le Cygne" by Camille Saint-Saens
PIANO, VIOLIN
(An uproarious duet, or duel, actually, dangerously competitive
and cunning. Not all that the composer had in mind, but still
striking.)

"Silbersterne" by Carl Pohm
PIANO
(A mazurka, an exercise in precision playing and shameless
showing off. Mistakes, when made, are plunged on and beaten
into submission.)

"Venetia" by J. S. Zamecnik
VIOLIN
(Old standard, stunningly done, the violin virtually soaring,
except for hitting ground twice or three times.)

"Watch Me Grow, Hear Me Flow" by David Banner Tally
GUITAR
(A solo, an exhibition of chord changes, an introduction to bar-
ring, sliding, and fingering. Not entirely successful.)

"None but the Lonely Heart" by P. I. Tschaikowsky
PIANO, GUITAR
(Attempting the classics. A good try.)

"You Tell Me Your Dream" by Charles N. Daniels
PIANO, GUITAR, VIOLIN
(Beginning as a duet, simple and sweet, and being visited zestfully
by the violin, all preening and proud. An exuberant display by
the three instruments, sloppy, triumphant, and interesting.)

ACT TWO

Scene One

"The Little Dog Waltz" by Frederick Chopin

Winter. Evening.

*Now the piano is in a private reverie, playing Bee-
thoven's Sonata* Pathétique. *The playing sounds
more forced than usual, not so confident.*

MARGARET MARY *is alone in the room, hovering
strangely over the piano, head cocked, concentrat-
ing. She wears a long dress, heavy sweater.*

*The room looks quite cheery, which is odd because
it is actually sloppier. There are now several great
piles of newspapers and magazines, and the whole
place could use a good dusting. The last trace of
light is in the sky.*

MARGARET MARY *errs, stops, glares at the key-
board, resumes with better success, negotiates a
few curves smoothly, then stops abruptly. She sits
for a moment, then gathers herself up. She reaches
beyond the piano and produces a walker, which
she leans on heavily. After a bit of adjusting she*

83

has the thing in place and she begins a turtle's walk across the room. Her posture has worsened alarmingly, there is less bounce to her step, but still her spirit is fiery. She stops at a lamp and turns it on.

The hallway door opens and ROBIN *enters, looking strange. She's gone flat, hair hanging limply, face made up plainly, clothes chosen for practicality. She wears slacks and a sweater that surely must have come from* MARGARET MARY's *closet. She carries a huge scrapbook.* MARGARET MARY *leans on her walker and reaches for her toes.* ROBIN *flips through a newspaper spread out on the table.*

ROBIN

It's supposed to snow again tonight. They say it's the worst winter in years. Every year they say that. Every one is the worst one. It's probably true. What are you supposed to do, huh?

(Looking at MARGARET MARY*)*

MARGARET MARY

My toe-touching exercises. They're made considerably easier with my portable balance beam.

ROBIN

Ah. Here. Listen to this: "Price of tin, after holding steady . . . up 21 *percent!* The sharpest rise . . ." It goes on, it goes on. "Bolivia . . . aluminum, *53* percent in a five-year period . . ." It blows me away. General Motors. Big business, big deal! You know?

*(*ROBIN *rips out a page, folds up the paper and carries it and several others to the mirrored door.*

She opens it and disappears inside. MARGARET
MARY *watches and wanders up to the table.* ROBIN
enters)

MARGARET MARY

Didn't see any rodents, did you?
(ROBIN *shakes her head. She tucks the article care-*
fully into the book)
Wouldn't be much room for them anyway with all the
newspapers. They'd be well-read rats, wouldn't they?
(ROBIN *doesn't respond. Her attention is focused*
on the scrapbook)
You know what we need? A paper drive! The Boy Scouts
in Iowa used to do it. They'd come round and take your old
newspapers and they'd use the money they'd get for them
to buy jackknives and hatchets, and other weapons. I'd say
we've got enough here to set them up with a Sherman tank
or something.
(She smiles at ROBIN, *but gets no response)*
Don't you think we might consider thinning our supply?
Libraries, you know, put them on microfilm. Robin?

ROBIN

Huh? Yeah, well, I'm weeding them out. It takes time.
There's so much to read I have trouble catching up.

MARGARET MARY

Well, it's not really normal to read the entire paper. It made
a great deal of sense when you concentrated on the theater
section.

ROBIN

I *read* the theater section, but it doesn't give a person any
real view of reality, does it?

MARGARET MARY

No, I suppose not. For a view of reality, you'd need to read Ann Landers or someone of that ilk.

ROBIN

There's interesting stories all through the paper. There's so much to know, it's very scary.
(She closes the book)
I have a whole collection here of very scary stories.

MARGARET MARY

Think I could look at it sometime?

ROBIN

Yip. Sometime. Not now.
(She busies herself with rearranging piles. MAR-GARET MARY watches, troubled)

MARGARET MARY

Have you had your dinner?

ROBIN

Hmm? I don't think so. I was going to make a sandwich, but I don't think I did.
(She squeezes her stomach)
Did you get some milk?

MARGARET MARY

What, dear?

ROBIN
(Loudly)
Did you get some milk?

MARGARET MARY

No, thank you. Oh, that's right, I was supposed to buy some. But I ran into that polio woman, Diffendal, from the thirteenth floor. She was just coming out of Gristedes on her walker, so I decided to race her home. Beat her by a mile. I always thought she dragged that thing. Looking for sympathy, I suppose. Well, she didn't get any from me today.

(She smiles at ROBIN, *pauses)*

Going out tonight?

ROBIN

Nope.

MARGARET MARY

Your friends must wonder what's the matter with you.

ROBIN

My friends have always wondered what's the matter with me.

MARGARET MARY

You should call them, go see them.

ROBIN

Margaret Mary, there's twenty feet of snow on the ground. I don't know any Eskimos. I'm perfectly happy here with you.

*(*MARGARET MARY *nods. She goes back to her exercises.* ROBIN *watches)*

I feel very close to you.

(No response)

I think you just hear what you want to hear.

(She watches a moment longer, then carries another pile of papers into the rat room)

87

MARGARET MARY

Have you thought about your acting class? Maybe enough time's gone by, you could try again without doing yourself any damage. Why not call and see if your forty-five dollars still counts.

(She looks up)

Oh. Never anyone home when it's time to talk turkey.

*(*ROBIN *emerges, looking at* MARGARET MARY *without comment.* MARGARET MARY *proceeds carefully)*

I met someone I think you might like.

ROBIN
(Warily)

Oh, yeah?

MARGARET MARY

He's a very nice young man, your age—around thirty. And he works at Lincoln Center in the library.

ROBIN

In the library? Is this person a librarian or something?

MARGARET MARY

Yes!

ROBIN

I'm throwing up.

(She heads into the kitchen)

MARGARET MARY

Well, he's very nice. I met him on the number thirty bus, so he's not rich, apparently, but very good-looking. And I'm positive he's one of us, straight as a board!

ROBIN
(Offstage)

Don't be too sure. They're pretty crafty, some of those types.

MARGARET MARY

No, no. I asked him several key questions and he answered them very masculinely.
(She smiles as ROBIN *enters, carrying a loaf of bread, a plate, a jar of peanut butter, a knife, and a banana)*
He said you should come down to the library, he'd show you around, take you to lunch.

ROBIN

Gee, that sounds just great, Margaret Mary. We can talk about the new encyclopedias.
(She half laughs, and sets her dinner on the table)

MARGARET MARY

Oh, stop it. I'm sure there are plenty of *fascinating* things to discuss with the librarian.
(She tries to think of some)
There's always the Dewey Decimal System.
(She laughs, pleased. ROBIN *laughs, too, in spite of herself)*
It could be lots of fun! What do you think?

ROBIN

I think *you* should have lunch with him.

MARGARET MARY

He didn't ask me.
(She smiles at ROBIN, *who busily constructs her sandwich)*

I see the Feast of Saint Gennaro has begun. Is there some correlation between the peanut butter and the bread and the banana? Or are they different courses?

ROBIN

It's a cabana sandwich. You spread the peanut butter on the bread, you slice the banana onto it, you place another piece of bread on top, and then you eat it.

MARGARET MARY

And then you say your prayers, I expect.
(ROBIN *stares at her. Pause*)

ROBIN

Did I ask you to pimp for me?

MARGARET MARY

I beg your pardon?

ROBIN

(A careful warning)
You better stop trying to manipulate me.

MARGARET MARY

Hmm?

ROBIN

Margaret Mary, the manipulator, that's you.

MARGARET MARY

What are you saying?

ROBIN

I'm saying you should behave yourself. Let people alone. I don't go out and arrange things for you. I don't go meeting men on buses and set them up with you. I've had enough men to last me, believe me. I went on a great binge when Peter Pan flew away, and what did it prove? Every man *stunk*. Who needs 'em? Maybe someday when I'm feeling charitable I'll go out and get one, and it ain't going to be a librarian.

(She glares at MARGARET MARY*)*

I'm mad at you, Margaret Mary.

MARGARET MARY

You seem mad.

ROBIN

I'm just trying to *live* my *life,* but, oh, no, that would be asking too much. There's always a mother popping up to make sure I don't get too good at it. I left one in Brooklyn, and I divorced another one. I don't *need* any more mothers. *Mothers* are *mothers!*

(She stands fuming at MARGARET MARY, *who considers what she's said)*

MARGARET MARY

You should listen to yourself sometime. You're starting to sound like Mr. Goo.

(The doorbell rings. ROBIN *stalks to the door, throws it open to reveal* SERGE*)*

ROBIN

Not now, Serge!

(She slams the door)

SERGE
(Offstage)

I understand.

91

ROBIN
(Marching back to MARGARET MARY*)*
Look, I don't have to stay here, you know. I can *quit.*

MARGARET MARY
(Taken aback)
I know that, of course.

ROBIN
So what if I like to read newspapers and clip things out and
put off my acting career for a little while and not waste time
crapping around with my dorko friends? So what? So
what?

MARGARET MARY
(Reasonably)
So. It doesn't seem very realistic to me, that's all.

ROBIN
Oh, is that right?

MARGARET MARY
It's just that I find you a very unusual girl and I would love
to see you challenge yourself a little bit. Realize some of
your potential. And not . . . sort of avoid reality.

ROBIN
You don't think I'm realistic, huh?

MARGARET MARY
Um. Well, no.

ROBIN
(Stung, she counterattacks)
Do you think *you're* realistic?

MARGARET MARY

What?

ROBIN

Holing up in this mausoleum apartment, never talking to anybody you don't feel like talking to . . .
(Shouting)
That ain't realistic, it's bulltinky! *You* should be like *me*. At least I'm honest. At least I *honestly* know I'm screwing up.

MARGARET MARY

What the hell are you talking about, Robin?

ROBIN

You know what you are? You're a user! You can't push me around like you do Cara. That makes you mad doesn't it?

MARGARET MARY

You're behaving like a real mutt, aren't you?

ROBIN

Well, shit. Excuse me. You're selfish, Margaret Mary. You're too selfish to reach out very far to anybody. You'd rather pay for it. Well, groovy for you. You can buy me for fifty dollars a week, and I can be bought, because I don't know what I'm doing maybe, but you don't own me, see, you only rent me, and you're not allowed to try to change me, that's not in the contract. So there! What do you think of that? I'll quit!

MARGARET MARY

So what do you think of this? I'll fire you.

ROBIN

Fine. Good. As you wish.

(MARGARET MARY turns, trips on her walker, and falls in an awful heap. ROBIN rushes to help her, but MARGARET MARY pushes her away. ROBIN storms through the hall door, as MARGARET MARY pulls herself up. After a moment, the entrance door opens and CARA enters, looking very downcast)

CARA

Hello.

(MARGARET MARY doesn't answer. ROBIN marches in, wearing a coat. MARGARET MARY watches her)

Hello.

(She smiles at ROBIN, who walks right past her, scowling at MARGARET MARY)

Hello.

(ROBIN doesn't answer. She heads for the entrance door)

MARGARET MARY

Where are you going?

ROBIN

I'm going *out*. Is that all right? Should I turn in my key?

MARGARET MARY

You didn't eat your dinner.

(ROBIN picks up the plate and thrusts it at CARA)

ROBIN

Here. Have a sandwich.

CARA

Thank you. Sure you don't want it?

(ROBIN doesn't respond. She proceeds to the door)

MARGARET MARY

Just a moment. I want to say something to you, just in case you develop hypothermia and die in a snowbank. I understand what you said to me, at least what I heard of it, and I understand why you said it. Now I want *you* to understand that I have great affection for you, and great concern, and the fact of the matter is you're becoming rather strange. And if it's true you don't know what you're doing, then I suggest you take a moment and find out. You better face up, dear. *If* you're determined to be mulish and stupid, then you'll have me to reckon with, unless of course you choose to take your business elsewhere. So you'd better hang onto your hat. I'll be damned if I'll sit by and watch you get stuck in the mud.

(They glare at each other, both angry, and hurt,
both wanting to say more, but unable to. Pause)
Well?

ROBIN

Well. So. I'm going now.

MARGARET MARY

Fine. Good. Go. Do as you wish.

ROBIN

Yeah. Well, I'll see you later, Margaret Mary.
(She starts to cry, turns)

MARGARET MARY

Robin.
(She can't think of anything profound to say)
You are a silly goose!

ROBIN

It takes one to know one!
                    (She exits, slamming the door)

CARA

Anything wrong?

MARGARET MARY

What is it, Cara?

CARA

She seems a little vexy. I wondered what her problem was.

MARGARET MARY

I think it comes from eating too many peanut butter and
banana sandwiches.
          *(*CARA *looks at the plate squeamishly and then sets
          it on the table)*
She needs to be kicked, kicked, kicked.

CARA

I'll say.

MARGARET MARY

Or she'll end up just like us.

CARA

What's wrong with us? Why is life so problematic, that's
what I don't understand. Last night we were supposed to
have a meeting of the tenants at eight-thirty. At eight José
locked the laundry room. He said he was under orders from
the owners. They didn't want us to have the meeting! Well,
we're going to file an official protest at our next meeting, if
we can find a place to have it. The niggardly boogers. Arctic

conditions outside and they turn off the heat for eight hours a day. Well, we're going to paint their wagons.

MARGARET MARY

Are you talking, Cara?

CARA
(Rushing to her)
Can't you hear me at all?
(Shouting)
Margaret Mary, Margaret Mary!

MARGARET MARY

What is it?

CARA

Shall I call a doctor? There's a dentist on the first floor, you know. And Dr. Cameron would come, I'm sure he would. Want me to call?

MARGARET MARY
(Firmly)

No, dear.

CARA

Son of a bitch! Son of a bitch! Son of a bitch!
(She sits, hides her face in her hands. MARGARET MARY turns, startled)
Ralphie is dead. My best friend, the cat. Dead prematurely—four years old. In the prime of his life. I got him for Mother on her ninetieth birthday. I thought she'd like a little fuzzy face smiling up at her, but I was wrong. She

97

started to sneeze and that got the whole thing off on the wrong foot. And then Adie Nims said she "didn't mind the cat." Fine! Good. Not minding and liking are two different things altogether, I've learned that much.

(The doorbell rings)

Adie Nims is a son of a bitch! Your doorbell's ringing.

(She heads for the door, holding up her hands)

He was only this small, he never got any bigger.

(She throws her hands)

Pfft! Dead! Four years old. What's the point? What's the point?

(She opens the door to reveal SERGE, *looking very worried)*

Not now, Serge.

(She slams the door)

SERGE
(Offstage)

I understand. Good-night.

CARA

Serge is the one who found him. On top of the ash cans. Right under 204. When we lived there, he used to crawl out in the summertime and climb down and chase the big roaches. Stupid Adie Nims keeps the kitchen window open all the time. I don't think she's totally with us. I suppose Ralphie was confused and thought he was just jumping down one flight, instead of seventeen. It might have been all right if he'd hit the snow, but no such luck.

(She looks at the door)

Serge was very nice about it. He said he'd take care of Ralphie.

MARGARET MARY

I'm sorry.

(She pulls herself up)

Have a bonbon.

CARA

Oh, thank you.
(She takes one, wipes her eyes)
Isn't life discouraging? There's never one thing you can cling to and say, "This is good, this will last." God forbid you should try feeling secure.
(She puts her face in her hands. MARGARET MARY *awkwardly places her hand on* CARA's *head. She pats her hair for a moment.* CARA *looks up appreciatively.* MARGARET MARY *stops)*

MARGARET MARY

Do you think I'm selfish?

CARA

What?

MARGARET MARY

Do you think I'm manipulative?

CARA

Oh, I wouldn't know about that sort of thing.

MARGARET MARY

Do you think I *use you?*

CARA

Use me? No. I wish you would, but you never do.

MARGARET MARY

I've never thought of myself as selfish. I suppose I am single-minded, and it's true people do tend to irritate me. I just assumed it was because I was superior to them. Or inferior, I've never been sure which.

CARA

Well, you have to squint your eyes when you look at people sometimes, or you'll never like what you see, that's what my mother said, and that's what I try to do. You have to give them salt, you know, and other things. It's like making soup. You know what I mean.

MARGARET MARY

No, I don't.

CARA

I've always liked you myself. I can't speak for anyone else, but I've always liked you.

MARGARET MARY

Why?

CARA

Well, because you have gusto, you know, and style.

MARGARET MARY

Mmm.
(She considers this; looks at the piano keys)
Well. Shall we play? Give ourselves a boost. Or are you in too much of a state?

CARA
(Getting her violin)
No, no. Music is a great tonic.

MARGARET MARY

It is. Have any preference? A nice waltz perhaps?

CARA

Doesn't matter. A waltz would be nice. You love your waltzes, don't you?

MARGARET MARY

I like waltzes all right. They're not quite as intelligent as fugues, I suppose, or sonatas, but they have their place. I like their simplicity. I think the waltz is a very neat form of music, very tidy. So precise. And logical. The Holy Trinity, the great triumvirates, the three branches of government, the pyramids. It's comforting, isn't it?

CARA

I guess so.

MARGARET MARY

Waltzes put me in a dreamy frame of mind. Sometimes I think I live my life in three-quarter time, and that I am alone in hearing the beat. I suppose people have been sent away for less. Sometimes I picture West Seventy-second Street as some snowy boulevard in Vienna a hundred years ago, the women dressed in long dresses, the men in high hats and tails, riding in sleighs, whispering along behind white horses, everyone vibrant and alive and full of humor and ideas. It's a considerable improvement over what I do see. No one ever *spits* in Vienna, or worse. I can *hear* the rhythm, I can *feel* the beat. This is helped now, of course, by walking on a walker. Clunk-two-three, clunk-two-three.

(She looks through her music)

CARA

I like some of the love songs myself. Some of the popular ones. That's what I grew up on. Mother had them all. Victor Herbert and Cole Porter, that crowd.

MARGARET MARY

Here's Chopin. Dear, dear Chopin. You know what's in here? The perfect thing.

(She flips the pages)

"The Little Dog Waltz." We'll play it for Ralphie.

CARA

Ralphie is a cat.

MARGARET MARY

Then we'll play it for ourselves. Ready?

(MARGARET MARY starts to play. CARA fails to join her. MARGARET MARY stops)

You missed the boat.

CARA

(Snapping)

I wasn't ready.

MARGARET MARY

Well, take your time.

CARA

I'm ready now.

(MARGARET MARY smiles and begins again. CARA slides in gracefully enough. They play smoothly for a moment. MARGARET MARY nods. CARA turns suddenly and yells at the wall)

Son of a bitch!

(She continues to play. MARGARET MARY smiles at her)

MARGARET MARY

Now we're cooking.

(The music continues)

Scene Two

"Wein, Weib, und Gesang" by Johann Strauss

Spring. Evening.

The music has gallumphed along. The violin has faded, the Chopin has faded, and now the piano is having a choppy go at Strauss.

The room is all sparkly and neat, clutter gone, vase of flowers adding rare color. On the dining table are laid out a handsome coffee percolator and a row of china cups, a pile of napkins, a pile of plates. Outside, the sky is just turning from pink to black.

MARGARET MARY *sits at the piano in a wheelchair. She wears a bright, strange dress and her hair sports a bow. She is playing with great concentration and she stumbles now and again, but even when she does it is with a certain lively boldness. Her touch is light and there is about her a look of excitement, a bounce to her movement.*

103

Suddenly the entrance door opens and CARA *bursts in, all aflutter. She is dressed in an outrageous pink gown, and she carries a Tupperware cake container containing a cake. She steps to the piano and swirls about in front of* MARGARET MARY, *who stops playing to gaze in amazement at her.*

MARGARET MARY

Cara! My word!

CARA

Do you think I look all right? Not too ostentatious, is it?

MARGARET MARY

Not at all. It's very *you,* Cara.

CARA

Thank you. I wanted to look right.
(She sets her cake on the table)
Oh! Will you look at what you've done here. It's so beautiful. Except you don't have enough cups and plates out.

MARGARET MARY
(She turns the chair)
Robin merely said she was "bringing a bunch of friends." She didn't say how big a bunch.

CARA

Well, we can always get more out if we have to.
(She looks about excitedly, as if picturing the room full of revelers, then proudly sets out her cake)
It's so exciting. Don't you just love parties?

MARGARET MARY

Not especially, no. But Robin's never asked to bring her friends home before, and I figure if she can extend herself that much, then so can I. It's part of my new personality: unselfish to a fault. Cara, could you do me a huge favor?

CARA

Of course, Margaret Mary.

MARGARET MARY

Robin seems to have left her underthings hanging by the kitchen window. Could you put them in her room?

CARA

No! She should put her things away herself.

MARGARET MARY

I quite agree. But she didn't. She was in such a wild rush tonight, and now there's no time, and I don't think bras and panties in the kitchen is the sort of image we should present to our guests.
(When CARA *doesn't move)*
Go on, dear, or I'll tell everyone they're yours and then the tongues will wag.
(This motivates CARA *to march into the kitchen and emerge with a coat hanger, from which hang bras and panties. She scowls at them)*

CARA

Look at these skimpy little things. I thought she didn't wear bras.
(She crosses to the hallway door and places the underthings out of sight)

MARGARET MARY

She does for special occasions, I believe. When she wants to keep up appearances.

CARA

If my mother was alive she'd tell me to keep my eyes open tonight for a good batch.

MARGARET MARY

Batch of what?

CARA

A *batch*. You know. Eligible *batch*. *Bachelor*. Not that I'd want one.

(The doorbell rings)

Oh, no. That stupid Ellen Diffendal! Mucked it up again!

(CARA opens the door and SERGE enters, wearing a strange jacket and mismatching slacks. His hands and face are well-scrubbed, hair slicked down. He carries a bag with two cans of beer)

Oh, Serge, it's only you.

SERGE

Hello, beautiful ladies.

CARA

(To MARGARET MARY)

Ellen Diffendal and Adie are stationed in the lobby and are going to call on the intercom the minute Robin and the guests arrive!

MARGARET MARY

What's the point of all that?

CARA

Nothing, nothing. Just having fun, that's all.

SERGE

How you are, Miss Elderdice?

MARGARET MARY

Well, I'm fine, Serge. Never better. Why didn't you bring your lovely wife?

SERGE

What for? Why spoil things.
(He sits on the sofa and opens a beer)
We are having some fun, aren't we? Is no nice to be here with my good friends. The first time ever I'm invited to a home and not to fix something.

MARGARET MARY

Well, actually there are a few little things that need looking into.

SERGE

Does not matter. Tonight I am only having so much fun with my friends.

MARGARET MARY

That's the spirit.
(The buzzer buzzes. CARA *springs into action)*

CARA

Bingo!
(She rushes to the door)

MARGARET MARY

What did she say?

SERGE

Bingo.

MARGARET MARY

I wonder if Cara is happy in her little world.

CARA

(Speaking into the intercom, holding the receiver to her ear)

Yes? Yes? Ellen? Adie? . . . My God!

(She shouts to MARGARET MARY)

Oh, my God, they're coming! They just got to the elevator. Robin and some of the others.

(Back to the intercom)

I'll talk to you later, Adie. I don't know how many. I've got to go, Adie, I've got to go.

(She hangs up, rushes to the mirror, starts primping furiously)

MARGARET MARY

Nervous, Cara?

CARA

(Loudly)

No! Of course not!

SERGE

Mrs. Varnum, never have I seen you so lovely. This lovely dress makes you fatness look so pretty.

(CARA looks at him, horrified, looks at the mirror, then rushes through the hallway door)

108

MARGARET MARY

Serge, you could have been a poet.

SERGE

I like the women so much. The men and the boys are so *lucky* to have the women.

MARGARET MARY

I'll say.

SERGE

You looking so pretty tonight. I think when you was young you was so beautiful.

MARGARET MARY

So I was told.

SERGE

I, too, look pretty tonight. And not smelling so much. Sometimes when I wear these pretty clothes, I tell me, "You could be a man in a store, or a bank manager, many things." I think I look so wonderful, certainly, but when I put on my working pants and my working shirt, I feel better. This is life.

(*The entrance door opens and in steps* ROBIN, *followed by* GLEN DABRINSKY. *He is thirty-four, reasonably handsome, an easy smile, and a most sincere manner. He is dressed fashionably and speaks with a bit of a New York accent.* ROBIN *has recouped some of her sparkle, and looks quite lovely, white straw hat and stunning dress, all flowers and cleavage*)

ROBIN

Hiya. Sorry we're a little late.

109

MARGARET MARY

Don't be silly. You're among the first to arrive.

ROBIN

Oh. Ha ha. You look lovely tonight, Margaret Mary.

MARGARET MARY

Thank you.

ROBIN
(She laughs nervously)

Um. This is Glen Dabrinsky. Glen, this is my friend, Margaret Mary.

MARGARET MARY
(Grandly, extending her hand)

Hello, so pleased you could come.

GLEN
(Shaking her hand, smiling)

The pleasure is mine, believe me. Good to be here.

MARGARET MARY

This is Serge . . . something or other.

SERGE

Barrescu. Barrescu.

MARGARET MARY

That's correct.

SERGE
(Grabbing GLEN's hand)

How you are?

GLEN

(Thinking he's being put on)

I'm fine. How *you* are?

SERGE

What?

(He grabs ROBIN)

Never have I seen you so beautiful. I could die.

ROBIN

Don't do that. Um. Excuse me. I gotta tinkle.

(She exits quickly)

MARGARET MARY

What did she say?

GLEN

(Embarrassed)

Um. I'm not sure.

SERGE

She say she got to tinkle.

MARGARET MARY

Oh. Well, so much for the female mystique. Wouldn't you like to sit down, gentlemen?

GLEN

I would love to.

(He sits on the sofa, where he is quickly joined by SERGE*)*

SERGE

So. You are from Europe?

111

GLEN
(Pleasantly)

Huh? No.

SERGE

Dabrinsky? You are from Russia. Or Poland.

GLEN

I'm from Montauk. My family was Russian.

SERGE

Oh. Okay. You are Communist?

GLEN

No, I'm a Libra. How about yourself?

SERGE

I spit on the Communists. Pfft!
(He makes a spitting motion at the floor, which
MARGARET MARY *regards with some consterna-*
tion)

MARGARET MARY

There's an art to being a hostess, which I'm afraid I've
never totally mastered.

GLEN

Ah, you're doing great, don't worry about it.

MARGARET MARY

All right, I won't.
(Pause. She searches for something to say)
What, um, what line of work are you in, Mr. Dabrinsky?

GLEN
(Almost apologetically)

I'm just a lawyer.

MARGARET MARY
(Trying hard)

A lawyer! Well. I should think that must be very interesting.

GLEN

Not really. I'm sort of an assistant to the assistant public defender.

MARGARET MARY

Well. Good for you. It sounds like you're on your way.

GLEN

Yeah. To somewhere. I don't know, it's tough. It seems like every time I go forward one step I go two steps back.

MARGARET MARY
(Can't help herself)

Perhaps you should try walking backwards.

GLEN
(After a moment he laughs)

That's very funny. You've got a great sense of humor.

MARGARET MARY

Do you think so?
(She's pleased)

113

GLEN

Yes. I think that's a great combination when an attractive person like yourself is also funny. I find that charming.

MARGARET MARY

Ah.

> *(She doesn't quite know what to make of this. A moment passes)*

GLEN

Oh, wow. I don't believe this piano. This is a *major* instrument, am I right?

MARGARET MARY

Yes.

GLEN

It's *just charming*. So Robin tells me you're a real crackerjack piano player.

MARGARET MARY

Oh, yes, very crackerjack.

GLEN

Well, there's nothing like music for soothing the old soul, is there?

MARGARET MARY

Particularly this old soul. Music is a wonderful tonic, as I often say.

GLEN

Let me ask you something and forgive me if I sound even remotely audacious.

114

MARGARET MARY

All right.

GLEN

Will you play for me? Sometime? I would really like that.

MARGARET MARY

Oh, well. I might, I guess.
                    (She smiles, charmed)
I'm not all that good anymore.

SERGE

Goddam liar! She is playing so beautiful could break my heart.

MARGARET MARY

Oh, thank you, Serge.
                    (She smiles at GLEN, *enjoying herself)*

GLEN

You have a wonderful smile, has anyone ever told you that?

MARGARET MARY

Not in the last several decades.

GLEN

Well, you do. Wonderful, warm. I can understand why Robin is so fond of you.

MARGARET MARY

Oh? Is she? Fond of me?

GLEN

That's what she told me, riding up in the elevator. She said you're her best friend.

115

MARGARET MARY

Oh. Well, yes. I guess we've been sort of growing together, in our own strange fashions.

GLEN

She's a wonderful person, isn't she?

MARGARET MARY

Oh, yes. Indeed. A real original. Intelligent, and *honest*.

GLEN

Very warm, very funny. A wonderful smile.

MARGARET MARY
(Thinking this sounds familiar somehow)
Um. Yes.

GLEN

She's charming. Very charming.

MARGARET MARY

Yes.

SERGE

So beautiful with no clothes.
*(*GLEN *and* MARGARET MARY *look at* SERGE*)*

MARGARET MARY

Yes. Well.
*(*CARA *enters, wearing a sweater over her gown)*

CARA

Don't look at me. You're looking at me. Margaret Mary, I've got one of your sweaters on, I hope you don't mind.

116

MARGARET MARY

Not at all. It looks lovely. Cara, this is Glen Dabrinsky, a very charming lawyer.

CARA

(Smiling nervously)

Oh. Well. Hello. Are you one of Robin's friends?

GLEN

Yes! Are you?

CARA

Oh, yes. We're very close. We're like sisters. Aren't we, Margaret Mary?

MARGARET MARY

What? No question about it. I have trouble telling them apart sometimes. Why don't we all sit down, those of us who aren't sitting already? I think parties work best when all the people are at the same level.

(GLEN *and* SERGE *return to the sofa.* CARA *hastens to sit near* GLEN)

CARA

(To GLEN, *demurely)*

How do you know Robin anyway? I can never understand how people meet anybody.

GLEN

Um. Actually we met on a bus.

MARGARET MARY

There's your answer. You need to take more buses.

117

CARA

(She looks at MARGARET MARY, *embarrassed, turns to* GLEN)
Why would a lawyer ride a bus?

GLEN

That sounds like a riddle. Why would a lawyer ride a bus?

CARA

Well, I mean, I just thought lawyers were supposed to be rich.

GLEN

That's what *I* thought. Till I became one. I've got to find some wealthier criminals.
(He smiles)

CARA

(Seriously)
Well, that shouldn't be too hard. What about politicians?

GLEN

(He laughs)
That's very funny. You're very funny.

CARA

I am?

GLEN

Yes. I'll bet you're somebody it would be a lot of fun to spend time with.

CARA
(Disarmed)

Oh, I guess I am, in a way.

GLEN
(He smiles at her sincerely, turns to MARGARET
MARY*)*

Don't you think she's funny?

MARGARET MARY

Oh, yes. Very funny.

GLEN
(To CARA*)*

And very pretty, too.

CARA
(Thrilled)

Oh, stop it.

GLEN

Look at that smile. That's a million-dollar smile.

CARA
(Flirting right back)

You big liar.

GLEN

Hey. I'm a lawyer—would I lie?
(He laughs, faces both ladies)
You know something? I'm glad I came tonight. I'll be hon-
est with you: I didn't want to come. I thought it would be

a drag. But you two are *great*. You're wonderful, I mean it.

(He turns to SERGE*)*

You're great, too.

*(*SERGE *raises his beer without comment)*

This is just great. I gotta tell you: I'm excited.

CARA

So are we! Aren't we, Margaret Mary?

MARGARET MARY

(Not quite as enthusiastic)

Yes.

GLEN

(Looking about)

Look! You've got your party stuff out. Beautiful, really beautiful. What's the occasion?

MARGARET MARY

Oh, just sort of a celebration. Of Robin's *metamorphosis*.

SERGE

Her what?

CARA

(Superiorly)

Metamorphosis.

MARGARET MARY

Yes. She went through a *slight* dormant period for a while and now it's *spring* and she's *metamorphosizing*.

(To GLEN*)*

I love that word, don't you?

120

GLEN

It's a beautiful word.

MARGARET MARY

We're very proud of our Robin. She's going out and meeting new friends. I just wish some of them had a better sense
of punctuality.
    (ROBIN *enters, looking refreshed. And nervous)*
Ah. Thank goodness. Here's our butterfly now.

ROBIN

Huh? Um. Hiya, everybody.

GLEN

Hi, Robin. You have got some very charming friends here.
Real sweethearts.

MARGARET MARY
(Cutting through it)
Robin, what time did you tell the others to be here?

CARA
(Exuberantly)
Yeah, where the heck is everybody? Let's get this thing
going!

ROBIN

Um. Ha ha. I guess there's nobody else coming.

CARA

What?

ROBIN

This is all you get.

What?

(She looks from GLEN *to* MARGARET MARY, *incredulous)*

One guest? What kind of party is this going to be?

MARGARET MARY

A small one, I'd say.

CARA

Oh, boy. What are we going to do now? I suppose everybody's supposed to talk to *him* and dance with *him* and everything?

GLEN

Don't knock it if you haven't tried it.

SERGE

Mrs. Varnum, *I* will dance with you.

CARA

No thank you. I should have known if it was Robin's party it would turn out strange.

(She looks quickly from ROBIN *to* GLEN *and back)*

Who is this character anyway?

GLEN

(Getting peeved)

Hey, Cara. Give us a break, kid.

CARA

(To GLEN*)*

What?

GLEN
(To CARA*)*

You're getting agitated.

CARA
(To ROBIN*)*

What is he—your boyfriend or something?

ROBIN
(Defensive outburst)

What's it to ya? Mind your own beeswax, for Christ's sake!
Jesus!

CARA

Well? Is he?

GLEN
(Raising his hand)

Guilty.

CARA

Oh. Well. Why didn't you tell us? What's the big secret?
Why'd you have to lie about it?

ROBIN
(Feeling cornered)

Who you calling a liar? Huh? It's no secret! You wanna
know? Okay, fine. Good. He wants us to live together!

MARGARET MARY

What did you say?

ROBIN

He's asked me to move in with him.

123

SERGE

You son of a bitch.

ROBIN

And, um, I guess I'm going to.
(A pause while the news sinks in. SERGE *and* CARA
look at MARGARET MARY *nervously, but she merely
stares at* ROBIN. *At last* CARA *goes to battle, marching to* ROBIN)

CARA

You've lost your gumballs, haven't you? You can't do that!

ROBIN

Why not?

CARA

You can't just go out and *do* whatever you want to in life.

ROBIN

Why not?

CARA

You just can't!

GLEN
(Trying for a joke)
I would say this party is taking a downward turn.

CARA
(Yelling)
Oh, shut up!

124

ROBIN
(Yelling)

You leave him alone!

GLEN

Yeah!

SERGE
(Enjoying himself)

Everybody is fighting!

CARA
(To ROBIN*)*

You deserter! Where's your sense of loyalty? Let me tell you something, young lady: *I* would never *betray* somebody just because I met some moron of a man!

GLEN
(Jumping up)

Hey! Are you calling me a moron? Huh? Did you mean me? I could sue you for that!

CARA

You just stay out of this!

GLEN
(Really peeved now)

Hey! Give me a break! I've gotta tell you: I don't like it here. There's a lot of *attitudes* in this room. I am not a moron. I'm just a very nice lawyer, and I'm trying real hard to be *nice* to everybody. Look. I've asked this woman to live with me, that's all. I love her, she's great. And it's nobody's business. And if you people don't like it, you can buzz off!

125

(A pause. Finally MARGARET MARY *smiles, a picture of composure)*

MARGARET MARY
Well, I don't think we'll buzz off exactly, thank you just the same. *I* think it's time for refreshments, now that we've all worked up an appetite. You're on the refreshment committee, aren't you, Cara? Why don't you cut your cake, and Robin can pour us some coffee, and we can get our celebration back on its course.
*(*ROBIN *and* CARA *do as they're told)*

CARA
Celebration, my foot.
(She cuts her cake with a vengeance. ROBIN *wipes her eyes, trying not to cry as she pours coffee)*
I was starting to think you were a halfway decent person, but boy, was I wrong! Poor Margaret Mary, all the trouble she's been to. Some friend you turned out to be!

MARGARET MARY
(Composure gone for a moment)
Shut up, Cara!
*(*ROBIN *carries the tray of coffee cups, and crashes into* GLEN, *who was trying to help)*

GLEN
Shit!

ROBIN
Shit!

CARA
Oh, no! Now look what you've done!

126

SERGE

Is making stains on the floor. Someone has to pay.
(The four of them stand helpless, looking to MAR-
GARET MARY *for guidance)*

MARGARET MARY

My, my, my, what a group. Cara, take the young man into
my room and give him one of Happy Harry's suits to wear.
Serge, get a rag, please, and clean up this mess. Robin,
maybe you could pour us some more coffee without spilling
any. Go on, all of you, don't stand there looking stupid.

CARA

Will you be okay, Margaret Mary?

MARGARET MARY

I'm sure I will be.
*(*CARA *and* GLEN *exit.* SERGE *disappears into the
kitchen. There is a long pause)*

ROBIN

Did you think I was going to stay here forever?

MARGARET MARY

Of course not, dear.
(She considers it)
I don't know what I thought. I feel as though I've failed in
some way.

ROBIN

You haven't.

MARGARET MARY

Oh, I know.

127

ROBIN

I did sort of lie about bringing home a bunch of friends.

MARGARET MARY

I can see that.

ROBIN

I didn't want to make it seem like Glen is the only one I have or anything. Even though he is.
(Pause)
I'm sorry I lied.

(MARGARET MARY studies ROBIN, who suddenly seems like a stranger to her. She shrugs, proceeds carefully)

MARGARET MARY

Now listen . . .
(She stops, then decides to forge on)
God forbid I should sound like a mother, but don't you think you might take some time and think this thing through—

ROBIN
(Interrupting)
No! If I don't go now, I might never get out!

MARGARET MARY

You make this sound like the West Side Home for Hopeless Women or something.

ROBIN

You know what I'm saying.

MARGARET MARY

No, I don't.

128

ROBIN
(An outburst)

Then think about it! Dammit!
*(*SERGE *starts to enter from the kitchen, changes his mind.* ROBIN *lowers her voice)*
It's your fault anyway.

MARGARET MARY

It is?

ROBIN

Yeah, sure. You're a very fascinating friend. You make it real easy to stay here. Real comfy.

MARGARET MARY

Comfy. Thank you.

ROBIN
(Pause. Trying to stay on the track)
Yeah. Well. You're the one who told me to go out and *challenge* myself. Don't you remember?

MARGARET MARY

I remember very clearly. And is that what you feel you're doing? Challenging yourself?

ROBIN
(Not wishing to focus too hard on what *she's doing)*
Well, *yeah.*
(Pause)
It's just time to move on, that's all.
(Pause. MARGARET MARY *waits)*
See, I feel like I'm ready now to go off and start a whole

129

new life. You know. And I'll be growing in all kinds of new ways and everything.

(Pause)

And Glen . . . is, like, my lover, you see.

MARGARET MARY

That I *do* understand. I may be losing a few of my faculties, but there's nothing wrong with my common sense or my memory.

(She stares at ROBIN*)*

I'm just afraid I don't get the point of this *particular* young man. He seems ever so slightly abstruse to me.

ROBIN

(Forceful)

That's because you never want to look for the virtues in anybody.

MARGARET MARY

Ah.

ROBIN

He's a good person, Margaret Mary. He's real smart. He knows all kinds of interesting things. And he makes me *feel good,* and female, and young.

MARGARET MARY

I see.

ROBIN

(She smiles)

He thinks I have a great sense of humor.

MARGARET MARY

I'm not surprised at that.

ROBIN

Yeah! And if you only got to know him you'd understand. We're going to have a real neat life out there on Long Island, in his condo.

(Defensive)

And I figure so what if we're not exactly perfect for each other? Huh? That's part of the deal, right? And, hey, I'm not that far away, I'll come see you all the time.

(They share a look. ROBIN *quickly breaks the mood)*

So, that's the story.

(Pause)

You don't think I'm chickenshit, do you?

MARGARET MARY

I beg your pardon?

ROBIN

I mean, do you think it makes me a failure not becoming a movie star and everything? Like I don't have courage.

MARGARET MARY

Oh, bother. I think it would take great courage to go and live on Long Island.

(Pause)

Let me just say *one* thing to you though, if I may. One doesn't get to make very many mistakes in life. So don't muck it up! Nothing could make me happier than for you to have what you want. So few of us do. Perhaps it *is* time for you to move on. Then fine, so be it. Just don't sell yourself short, dammit!

ROBIN

Well, I won't.

(Pause. Nothing more to say)
Um. Cara's wrong, isn't she? I'm not deserting you.

Don't be silly.

You're going to be okay, aren't you?

Of course.

(Pause. Getting teary)
Will you miss me?

Very much.
> *(ROBIN falls against her, hugging her. MARGARET MARY hesitates, then hugs her, too. A moment passes. GLEN enters, wearing a bright suit, too large for him. CARA follows)*

Well! Happy Harry knew how to dress, didn't he?
> *(ROBIN stands and steps to GLEN)*

I look like I sell televisions, don't I?
> *(She hugs him, hides against his chest. MARGARET MARY watches for a moment, then looks at CARA, who also has been watching)*

Well, Cara? Shall we play?

132

*(She turns to the piano and begins playing
"Wein, Weib, und Gesang." CARA seems a bit
dazed, but she finds her violin and joins in. GLEN
rocks ROBIN gently to the music. He slowly leads
her into a little dance, as SERGE steps out of the
kitchen. When he realizes what's happening, he
sets down his rag and bucket, and dances alongside
the others, trying to keep pace. After a moment,
GLEN turns ROBIN to SERGE, who grabs her and
leads her into a dizzying waltz. CARA looks on dis-
approvingly. GLEN steps to her, takes her violin
and sets it down. She is horrified as he takes her
hand and begins to dance with her, but she virtually melts into his arms. MARGARET MARY
watches over her shoulder. Now her playing is
powerful, thrilling. The dancers keep pace. CARA
smiles shyly at GLEN, who smiles back, then looks
at ROBIN; she turns from SERGE's intense gaze and
smiles at GLEN. She nods. MARGARET MARY looks
from one to the next. She nods)*

Now we're cooking.

(The music continues)

SCENE THREE

"ONE MORE WALTZ" BY DOROTHY FIELDS AND JIMMY McHUGH

Fall. Afternoon.

The music has stopped. The room is shadowy and cold, uninhabited save for MARGARET MARY'S *shiny wheelchair parked at a strange angle near the rat room door. A window is open, its curtain dancing eerily in the autumn breeze. Something wrong here.*

A moment passes. The buzzer buzzes. No response. The entrance door opens and CARA *enters quietly. She is dressed in an impossible winter coat with matching hat, and she carries a large shopping bag. She squints into the gloom, spots the open window, drops her bag on the piano.*

CARA

Oh, bother. Bother, bother.
            (She wrestles with the window)
That stupid woman! Tsk. Unh. Unh!

135

(At last it closes. She turns on a lamp or two, looks about, sees the empty wheelchair, stares at it, confused, then rushes to the hallway door)
Margaret Mary! Margaret Mary!
(No answer. She exits. Doors bang offstage, CARA *calls, frantically)*

MARGARET MARY
(Offstage)
What is it?

CARA
(Offstage)
Margaret Mary! Margaret . . .

MARGARET MARY
(Crawling into view in the rat room doorway)
Cara! I'm right here. For God's sake!

CARA
(Rushing into the living room)
Margaret Mary? Margaret Mary?

MARGARET MARY
I do wish you'd stop shouting my name.

CARA
(Running to the rat room door)
Margaret Mary!
(Catching herself)
I'm sorry.

MARGARET MARY
I don't suppose you'd care to give me a lift, would you?

136

CARA

Of course.

(She tries to yank her up)

MARGARET MARY

Ouch! For God's sake. Let's not break all my bones at once.

CARA

(Setting her as carefully as she can into the wheel-chair)

I'm sorry. I'm so sorry. Did I hurt you?

MARGARET MARY

Don't worry about it. A lot of people take pleasure in abusing the handicapped.

(She arranges herself in the chair)

CARA

Oh, dear. I'm sorry. I was a little overanxious. Where's Mrs. Donaldson anyway?

MARGARET MARY

I fired her.

CARA

What for?

MARGARET MARY

Overanxiousness.

CARA

What? What do you mean?

137

MARGARET MARY

She took her job too seriously. There's nothing more depressing than a serious nurse.

CARA

(She studies MARGARET MARY, *who is more crippled than ever, her shoulders bent, her fingers curled grotesquely)*
Why did you get out of your chair?

MARGARET MARY

It wouldn't fit through the rat room door.

CARA

But what were you doing in the rat room anyway?

MARGARET MARY

I was cleaning it, dear.

CARA

Why?

MARGARET MARY

It was dirty. Unfortunately, once I got down, there was no getting back up.

CARA

Oh, my. How long have you been lying in there?

MARGARET MARY

I don't know. What day is it?

CARA

Oh, stop. I saw Mrs. Donaldson only a few hours ago . . .

on her way out! And you've been in there all this time, alone and cold. You poor thing.

MARGARET MARY

It hasn't been all that bad really. After I finished cleaning the floor, I had a very nice nap.
(She smiles at CARA*)*
I'm glad you came along though, before the rats got me.

CARA

Um. Do you want me to call the agency? I'm sure I can get them to send that stupid Mrs. Donaldson back.

MARGARET MARY

I don't *want* stupid Mrs. Donaldson back, thank you just the same.

CARA

Then I'll ask for a new one.

MARGARET MARY
(Emphatically)
No, dear! Thank you! Now look: The idiot has closed my window, trying to asphyxiate me, I suppose.
(She rolls to it. CARA *watches nervously, then pursues her)*

CARA

Margaret Mary, you can't keep firing your nurses! That's three now, in two months. You're going to get a reputation!

MARGARET MARY

Good! I don't care what I get just so long as it's not another *stupid nurse!* Do you understand? I don't *need* a stupid nurse . . .

(But she can't finish the thought because the window is closed tight and MARGARET MARY's *poor fingers can't manage it. She drops her hands, disgusted.* CARA *reaches over her carefully and opens the window, then steps away)*

Perhaps later, Cara. Call them later.

(She tries to peer out the window, calming herself)

I haven't seen Mr. Goo at all today. I hope she's all right.

CARA

I saw her. She had your coat on.

MARGARET MARY

How wonderful! How did it look?

CARA

(Cautiously sarcastic)

It goes real nice with her sneakers.

MARGARET MARY

I'm so pleased.

(She smiles and turns away from the window)

I don't recall leaving a hideous shopping bag on my piano.

CARA

(Rushing to remove it)

I'm sorry. It's mine. Look.

(She takes out a bright box, and from it a silky negligee, which is lovely, if a bit garish. When she holds it up it's immediately apparent that she is bigger than it)

What do you think?

140

MARGARET MARY

Um. It seems a bit small.

CARA

It's not for me, silly. It's for Robin. It's her wedding present.

MARGARET MARY
(Noncommittal)

Ah.

CARA

Have you gotten her anything yet?

MARGARET MARY

No. Actually I haven't.

CARA

You can go halvsies on this if you want.

MARGARET MARY

No. I really don't think I want to give Robin half a negligee, thanks just the same.

CARA

Well, you've got to give her something.

MARGARET MARY

Yes.
(She thinks about ROBIN *for a moment, sadly at first, then she smiles)*
I would like to. Mrs. Donaldson wouldn't *let me go* shopping, the silly bitch.

141

CARA

Well, it has been awfully cold out, you know.

MARGARET MARY

Why do certain people feel they have to go around deciding it's *too cold* for other people? I'd *like* to think that if I went outside and it was, say, fifty below zero, I might have the sense to come back in again. I really don't envision myself freezing to death in Needle Park.
(She's grown rather passionate by the end of this.
CARA *is suitably impressed)*

CARA

I could take you out. Tomorrow. If you wanted.

MARGARET MARY
(Pleased)

Could you? How nice.
(Pause)
We'll see. Let's see if we're all still alive tomorrow.
(She covers her face suddenly. A moment passes)

CARA
(Trying to brighten the mood)

Um. Oh, I meant to tell you! You made Ellen Diffendal's day, you made her *life,* letting her come up here to visit, and talking to her and everything. All the other ladies in the lobby are just about black with envy. They all said they never suspected Mrs. Elderdice was so nice, and I said, "Well, you don't know the half of it. Margaret Mary Elderdice is a *dove.* She's so sweet and attractive, and she just soars above the problems of life. She's a dove." All the ladies in the lobby loved that.

MARGARET MARY

Tell them not to look up when I fly over.
(Pause. The buzzer sounds)

CARA

Oh. Bingo!
(She opens the door, and SERGE enters, looking strangely downcast)
Oh, Serge, it's only you.

SERGE

Hello, beautiful ladies. Miss Elderdice, how you are?

MARGARET MARY

Pretty sparkly. How about yourself? No calamities?

SERGE

Thank you.
(He tries to smile, but can't quite. MARGARET MARY jumps in)

MARGARET MARY

Serge. I'm so glad you're here. Do you suppose you could look in the rat room? I had an opportunity this afternoon to study the floor very closely, and I wondered if perhaps the rats might not be pushing the grating out of the way, and then putting it back in place once they've gotten in. They're awfully clever, you know.
(She looks at SERGE, who stares thoughtfully toward the rat room)
Although I'm not sure they're really bright enough to handle a screwdriver. Perhaps you could take a look.

143

(When he doesn't move)
Or perhaps not, if you don't feel like it.
(She looks quizzically at CARA, *who shrugs)*

SERGE

I am no longer the super.

MARGARET MARY

What?

SERGE

I am fired.

CARA

What?

SERGE

Is funny. The broiler all the time is cold and sick. I try to fix, but is impossible. Too old. Instead of a new broiler, a new super. This is life.

MARGARET MARY

This is ridiculous.

CARA

It's an outrage, that's what it is! I'm going to tell the tenants' association, and we're going to take action!
(She steps to SERGE*)*
Don't you worry about a thing, this is all going to work out fine.

> *(She pats his arm gently. He is touched.* MAR-
> GARET MARY *watches, impressed)*

SERGE

Mrs. Varnum, thank you, no. I am finish. Is not fun being
not wanted. So, I go.

(Pause. He shrugs)

My fat wife has the brother in Pittsburgh, in Pennsylvania.
Always he wants me to work with him, making broken cars.

MARGARET MARY

What a good idea.

SERGE

Yes. Maybe. The brother, he say Pittsburgh is very beautiful.

MARGARET MARY

Well, I wouldn't go that far, but, why not? Give it a try.

SERGE

It would make my wife so happy, which is nice, I think.

CARA

Sure!

(A moment passes. SERGE seems to feel better.
MARGARET MARY smiles)

MARGARET MARY

Cara, get my purse, would you? We'll give Serge twenty
dollars.

SERGE

(Upset)

What? No, thank you. I don't want twenty dollars!

MARGARET MARY

Well, don't you see, if you're not going to be here at Christmas, this will be an early tip, that's all.

SERGE

I am not here being the super wanting Christmas tips.
(He pulls out his wallet and opens it)
See? I have money, too. Plenty money.
(He takes out two bills)
Here! Twenty dollars for Miss Elderdice, twenty dollars for Mrs. Varnum!
(He throws the bills in the air)
I am so sick of doing this and doing that for people not caring. People I think was friends and only are wanting something. Next time I fix toilet is my toilet. And the people can go fucking!

CARA

Hey!
(A moment passes)

MARGARET MARY

Well. I think that's a very good attitude. You're absolutely right.
(She smiles at SERGE)
Give me the money, Cara.
(CARA hands it to her. MARGARET MARY wheels to SERGE)
Here, Serge. I've insulted you, and I'm sorry. Forgive me. We're all friends here, such as we are. Come on, take the money. You can show your wife a good time in Pittsburgh, if that's not too contradictory.
(SERGE hesitates, then takes the bills, returns them to his wallet)

146

Now, sit down, please. I feel like a child, everything always going on over my head.

(SERGE sits, smiles at MARGARET MARY)

SERGE

Miss Elderdice, you I will miss the most. And Mrs. Varnum. Always so nice to me.

MARGARET MARY

Well, we'll miss you, too, dear.

CARA

You can come back and visit us sometime.

SERGE

Thank you.

MARGARET MARY

I think we should *celebrate* this new development. Why not get your wife and bring her up this evening for a cup of tea, and a little cheerful music?

SERGE

Um. I have not told her I am fired. Maybe she will kill me.

MARGARET MARY

Well, if she doesn't, then come back and bring her with you. Run along now and tell her, dear.

(He stands, hesitates)

Come on! Let's see that famous Barrescu smile.

(He smiles like a child)

What a handsome devil. Run along now.

147

SERGE

(At the door, emotionally)

Good-bye. Good-bye, my *friends.*

(He exits. MARGARET MARY *turns away.* CARA
watches her uncomfortably)

CARA

Um. Um. Would you like me to call the agency now and
get a new nurse? I could tell them we want someone a little
more like us, you know, intelligent and all.

MARGARET MARY

Um. Oh, dear. Um. Later. Tomorrow, Cara. It's so peace-
ful not having one.

*(Pause. She wheels herself to the piano, stares at
it, then turns to* CARA*)*

Why don't you play for me, dear? A little entertainment to
give our spirits a boost.

CARA

Well, I'd be happy to, I'm sure. Of course, Margaret Mary.
Whatever you'd like to hear. That I can play, I mean.

*(She rushes to get her violin and music. She smiles
at* MARGARET MARY*)*

Are you comfy there?

MARGARET MARY

Um. No. I really think I should lie down.

(She wheels to the sofa. CARA *stands nearby,
timidly, as* MARGARET MARY *tries to lift herself,
then drops back into the chair)*

I'm awfully sorry, but I'm going to have to ask you for a
lift again.

148

CARA

Well, I'd be happy to help you, Margaret Mary.
(She grabs her too enthusiastically)

MARGARET MARY

Ouch! For God's sake, Cara! Put me down, put me down!
(CARA lowers her back into the chair)

CARA

I'm sorry.

MARGARET MARY

If you'd like to try again, I can give you instructions, which
you must follow very closely, or I'll have to report you to
the S.P.C.A. Now, we'll put my arms on your shoulders,
like this.
(She does so)
And you reach behind me like this.
(She puts CARA's arms under hers)
And lift! Gently, gently, up we go. Good, good!
*(CARA lifts her carefully, holds her upright for a
moment)*
How do you like dancing class so far?
(CARA starts to giggle, thinks better of it)
And now, you just sort of fold me on the couch, that's good.
Legs, mm-hmm, and back, good. Pillow for the head. Very
good. Mother would be proud.
*(CARA follow the instructions to a T, gently and
lovingly)*
Aren't you strong! Very good, Cara. Thank you. What a lot
of fun. All right. Good! Ready for the concert.
(She smiles at CARA, who retrieves her violin)

149

CARA

Guess what. I'm moving.

MARGARET MARY

What?

CARA

Yes. There's a single coming up on eleven, because old Mrs. Mattolin is going into a home, and I've asked the managers, and I can have the apartment.

MARGARET MARY

What about your roommate, Adie Nims?

CARA

I'm sick of Adie Nims. Plus I've never been *alone* in my whole life. And you make it look like so much fun.

MARGARET MARY

Oh, it is. A laugh a minute.

CARA

Well, I'm going to try it.

MARGARET MARY

Good for you!

CARA

Yes. Um . . .
(Picking up a music book)
How about the "Gypsy Love Song"?

MARGARET MARY

The what?

150

CARA

"Gypsy Love Song." You know. Victor Herbert. One of Mother's favorites.
(She sings)
"Slumber on, my little gypsy sweetheart . . ."
(She stops)
That sound all right?

MARGARET MARY

It's not what we had in mind. How about a waltz of some sort? Put us in a dreamy frame of mind. Get the Strauss book, or the Chopin.

CARA

You don't like Victor Herbert?

MARGARET MARY

I don't have anything against him.
(Testily)
I would like to hear a waltz is all.

CARA

(Testily)
Well, let's don't get vexy!
(She stares at MARGARET MARY, *flustered but determined.* MARGARET MARY, *for her part, stares right back, enjoying the confrontation)*

MARGARET MARY

Vexy? Me?

CARA

By the way, if you *feel* like it, I thought you might help me with my campaign speech sometime. I mean, it's only my

151

greatest hour, my zenith, I suppose you might say. I wouldn't want the tenants' association to think they had a moron running for vice president.

MARGARET MARY

No, that would be a crime. Although we all know it has happened before.
(She realizes that this is not a laughing matter for
CARA*)*
I'd be honored to be your speechwriter. We'll give 'em hell, Cara.
(She studies her)
You really enjoy your little group, don't you?

CARA

It's all right. I like to feel that I'm doing something useful, you know, and that people like me. That's all. And if they don't like me—too bad.

MARGARET MARY
(Laughing)
You really are a wonder, Cara.

CARA

A wonder? A wonder? I just wonder what you mean by that.

MARGARET MARY
(Ever so slightly irritated)
You're a wonder, Cara. A marvel. I find you wondrous. I marvel at your verve and your feistiness and your resilience.
(Pause)
I'm giving you a compliment, you silly goose.

CARA

Oh! Yes. Thank you. Nice of you to notice. You're quite a
dove yourself.

MARGARET MARY

There's no need to reciprocate. We all know what a delight
I am. Now where's my waltz? I'm waiting for my waltz.

CARA

Oh, well. Um. Here's "One More Waltz." I guess that
qualifies as a waltz, doesn't it? It's from a movie which
you've probably never seen. *Love in the Rough,* starring
Robert Montgomery and Dorothy Jordan.
(She holds up the cover)
See? There they are, waltzing away.

MARGARET MARY

God help us.
*(CARA begins to play, quite prettily, then botches
it, shakes her head angrily, resumes with a choppy
flair)*
It could be worse.

CARA
(Stopping)

What?

MARGARET MARY

I say, it could be worse. Carry on.

CARA
(Indignant)

I can play something else if you'd rather.

153

MARGARET MARY

Not at all. We try to be open-minded. Come on, there'll be
no more interruptions, I promise. On with the recital.

(CARA *starts to play again*)

Cara. Cara.

CARA

(Getting irritated, she stops)

Yes?

MARGARET MARY

When you're finished, why not go up and get your toothbrush and come back and spend the night?

CARA

What did you say?

MARGARET MARY

I said when you're finished why not go up and get your
toothbrush and come back and spend the night.

CARA

You mean you want me to . . .

MARGARET MARY

You can have Robin's room, unless Mrs. Donaldson has
stolen the bed.

CARA

Well I . . .

MARGARET MARY

Why not? Give it a try.

Yes! Why not?

Good. All right then.
> *(They share a long, silly look.* MARGARET MARY
> *shrugs, and then waves her hand royally)*

Music!
> *(*CARA, *beaming, plays and sings sweetly)*

"One more waltz, here in my arms, close to my heart—"

Now we're cooking.

"One more dream, for me to dream . . ."
> *(The music continues)*

CURTAIN